W9-CMI-392

Practical Approaches

or Teaching Reading and Writing in Middle Schools

Teresa M. Morretta
Jenkintown Elementary School
Jenkintown, Pennsylvania, USA

Michelle Ambrosini
Maternity of the Blessed Virgin Mary School
Philadelphia, Pennsylvania, USA

INTERNATIONAL
**Reading
Association**

800 Barksdale Road, PO Box 8139
Newark, Delaware 19714-8139, USA
www.reading.org

The International Reading Association attempts, through its publications, to provide a forum for a wide spectrum of opinions on reading. This policy permits divergent viewpoints without implying the endorsement of the Association.

Director of Publications   Joan M. Irwin
Assistant Director of Publications   Jeanette K. Moss
Editor in Chief, Books   Matthew W. Baker
Permissions Editor   Janet S. Parrack
Associate Editor   Tori Mello
Publications Coordinator   Beth Doughty
Association Editor   David K. Roberts
Production Department Manager   Iona Sauscermen
Art Director   Boni Nash
Senior Electronic Publishing Specialist   Anette Schütz-Ruff
Electronic Publishing Specialist   Cheryl J. Strum
Electronic Publishing Assistant   Jeanine K. McGann

Project Editors   Matthew W. Baker and Sarah Rutigliano

Photo Credits   Cover: Jonathan A. Meyers, JAM Photography

Library of Congress Cataloging in Publication Data
   Morretta, Teresa M.
   Practical approaches for teaching reading and writing in middle schools/Teresa M. Morretta, Michele Ambrosini.
     p.   cm.
   Includes bibliographical references (p.) and index.
ISBN 0-87207-266-5
   1. Reading (Middle school)—United States.   2. English language—Composition and exercises—Study and teaching (Middle school)—United States.   I. Ambrosini, Michele.   II. Title.
LB1632.M63   2000   00-027277
428.4'0712—dc21

Dedication

To Joey, my brother and hero, for being my "teacher" in both my private
and professional life.

To all my past students who inspired and taught me how to be
a better teacher.

In loving memory of Hugo and Mary Morretta and Bessie Luczyscyn.

T.M.M.

To Nicholas and Dorina Ambrosini, my parents and best teachers,
for your love, support, and example.

To all my students, past and present, for teaching me and inspiring me to
want to write this book.

M.A.

Contents

Preface

Because of the lack of enthusiasm we began to feel as teachers of reading and writing in middle school, we searched for ways to invigorate ourselves, our classrooms, and our students. This search took many forms. We both studied for our master's degrees; belonged to professional organizations such as the International Reading Association, National Council of Teachers of English, and Association for Supervision and Curriculum Development; attended workshops; and read extensively about the teaching of reading and writing.

Teresa has taught sixth-grade reading and writing for 18 years. She began teaching reading using a basal reader and teaching writing using a grammar book, but her students barely read real literature or wrote for authentic purposes. Teresa personally valued talking about books, but she did not hear these conversations about literature in her classroom. She realized that the conversations were absent because the basal readers provided contrived selections to read. "Writing" was merely memorizing English grammar rules. How could a classroom be alive and dynamic when the teacher was not excited about the components of her program? Recognizing that her current practices were not effective, Teresa took action. She began reading the works of Graves, Atwell, Murray, and Routman, among others. She completed her master's degree at LaSalle University and attended the Pennsylvania Writing Project and the Pennsylvania Literature Project. She took what she learned and put it into practice a piece at a time, creating a dynamic learning environment. Today, Teresa and her students talk about books, suggest books to each other, write for authentic audiences, and become published authors—a community of readers and writers.

Michelle has taught seventh-grade reading and writing for 7 years. She began using an anthology that included excerpts from real literature and integrated writing, but student choice and active learning were missing. How could this reading and writing classroom become active and allow for students' choices? As she searched for an answer, she talked to Teresa—her mentor—who suggested professional readings and shared her practices. Michelle began to include various practices that engaged readers and writers. Teresa and Michelle then began to collaborate, creating a balanced reading and writing program for both sixth- and seventh-grade students. Michelle studied for her master's degree with a concentration on reading, writing, and literacy at the University of Pennsylvania. Now, she and her students also talk about and suggest books, write for authentic audiences, and become published authors.

Together, we continued to refine our program. Because our classrooms are thriving as communities of readers and writers, we wanted to share this accomplishment with fellow teachers. We envision our book as a resource for educators who want to find practical approaches for teaching reading and writing in middle school classrooms. We believe that our purpose as teachers of reading and writing is to enable students to become lifelong readers, writers, and learners. It is also our belief that a teacher should have his or her own philosophy of language learning that incorporates many approaches; this is accomplished by educating oneself through professional literature and by reflecting on one's practices. This book demonstrates our approach to teaching reading and writing that has developed from our professional reading and our reflections on our practical experiences in the classroom. Our philosophy of language learning evolved into our eclectic approach—a combined approach—embracing aspects of both explicit instruction and whole language.

Our text is designed for novice and veteran teachers who need a starting point to begin the transition to the combined approach to teaching reading and writing in middle school. The book provides discussion of the components essential to a balanced reading and writing classroom. For the sake of clarity, we separate reading into its own chapter and writing into another chapter. We do believe, however, as *The Pennsylvania Framework for Reading, Writing and Talking Across the Curriculum* (Lytle & Botel, 1996) informs us, that reading and writing are interrelated meaning-making, language-based processes that "enhance" each other (p. 6).

In Chapter 1 we define explicit instruction and whole language. We then discuss how our combined approach to teaching language to middle school students embraces aspects of both explicit instruction and whole language. A discussion of the adolescent learner also is included to show the reader how language learning in this context differs from language learning at the elementary or secondary levels. Throughout the chapters, the approaches support developmentally appropriate practices for young adolescents.

Chapter 2 presents our recipe for success. A key resource that we cite throughout this chapter is *Standards for the English Language Arts* (1996) developed by the International Reading Association (IRA) and the National Council of Teachers of English (NCTE). These standards provide suggestions for inspiring lifelong readers, writers, and learners, and they match our goals for creating a dynamic reading and writing classroom. We give examples of how each standard comes to life in our classrooms—snapshots of essential elements of a reading and writing classroom. These essential elements are discussed and practical approaches that teachers can utilize are offered in greater detail in Chapters 3 and 4.

In Chapter 3, practical approaches to engage readers—sustained silent reading, dialogue journals, double entry journals, reading/writing workshop, and literature circles—are delineated. We include a weekly overview to demonstrate how we manage the various approaches in the reading and writing classroom. Less complex approaches appear first, and those requiring more preparation follow. For each approach, we include a student definition, our explanations, student examples, and a rationale to show its value in the classroom.

Chapter 4 offers practical approaches to engage writers—freewriting, minilessons to teach writing, conferencing and assessment, spelling workshop, and revisiting reading/writing workshop. Again each approach is explained using student definitions and examples, our discussions, and rationales.

In Chapter 5 we describe how the reading and writing connection is celebrated in our classrooms and explain the activities we include to accomplish this celebration—portfolios, poetry workshop, blank books, and author studies.

The appendixes provide readers with sample lessons using literature circles, literature-circle role assignments, reader-response journal questions, various teacher- and student-reflection sheets, and a writing rubric. Throughout the book, assessment is discussed and rubrics are provided for the approaches when warranted.

A middle school teacher must create a classroom environment in which students engage in meaningful learning and recognize the connection between reading and writing. The following chapters include the components that support a balanced reading/writing classroom and inspire lifelong readers, writers, and learners.

Acknowledgments

I would like to acknowledge my parents, who were my first teachers, meeting my every need and inspiring me as a learner.

To my professors at LaSalle University, Dr. Bob Vogel and Dr. Preston Feden, thank you for giving me a sound foundation.

I began my career as an educator with the support of John Mostak and Sister Bonita Smith, both whom encouraged my professional growth, and Anne Hipp, a teacher consultant, whose never-ending support and encouragement gave me the courage to explore the field of education. Janine Giuliano and John Saunders, my friends and colleagues, your love and friendship mean the world to me.

I thank my current principal, Doris Grove, for her encouragement; she is my biggest supporter.

Michelle Ambrosini, my colleague and friend, believed in me and shared my excitement for teaching reading and writing to middle school students.

To Hallee Zaslavsky, our personal editor, thanks for all your time and your interest in our endeavors.

Michael Weaver, our technology expert, your help made our book possible.

Rosemary and Natalie, thank you for your love and friendship.

Last but not least, thank you to my husband, Louis Strupczewski, who truly believes in me—my talents and skills—more so than I do!

Teresa M. Morretta

I am lucky to have had the guidance and support of many people who encouraged me to be the best teacher and person I can be.

First, I thank the teachers who were my role models. John McCabe knew years before I did that I was meant to be a teacher and was not insulted when I said, "No way." John Mostak and Betsy Maloney taught me more about being a teacher than any book. Teresa Morretta, my mentor, single-handedly shaped the teacher I am, but more important, her friendship and guidance have made me a better person.

I appreciate the support and guidance of Sister Bonita Smith and Kathleen Veasy for serving as principals who have encouraged and appreciated the decisions I have made in my classroom for my students.

My friends and fellow teachers—Tricia Adolph, Patti Costello, Mary Gelovich, Sue Hanson, and Megan Simpson, thank you for sharing my joy for teaching, for your professionalism, and for your encouragement.

My grandparents—Biagio and Assunta Ambrosini and Raffaele and Esterina Petretta, you continue to teach me about hard work and love me unconditionally.

Danielle, Nicole, and Michael, my best friends, this is more worthwhile because I have you to share this celebration.

Michelle Ambrosini

We would both like to thank the International Reading Association for the opportunity to share our philosophy and love for teaching reading and writing to middle school students.

We appreciate the tremendous time and effort of Matt Baker. We could not have done this without his guidance.

CHAPTER I

Reading and Writing in Middle School: What We Learned From Research and Where It Took Us

The "correct" philosophy of language learning and instruction has been a hotbed of debate for years. Policy makers, school boards, parents, and the media have generated opinions about language learning and have disseminated them. These diverse opinions have influenced educational policies and muddled what constitutes effective instruction. The real experts are in the classroom—teachers and students.

To untangle this chaos surrounding effective instruction, teachers must recognize and assume their roles and responsibilities to be active learners themselves. When teachers are active in their own learning about education, they are empowered to affect student learning. Teachers begin this process by reading professional books and journals; by attending conferences, workshops, inservices, and summer institutes; and by visiting other teachers' classrooms. As teachers gain knowledge about language learning, they relinquish the safety of using only teachers' guides, worksheets, and curriculum guidelines, which then become resources, not remedies, for instruction.

Middle school students pose additional challenges for teachers as they design instruction. Until the 1990s, these students were largely ignored by teacher training programs that focused on elementary or secondary education. This inattention to young adolescents put teachers as well as students at a disadvantage. It became apparent that for teachers of middle school students to design developmentally appropriate practices for effective language instruction, they must study both language learning and adolescent development.

Our classroom experiences with adolescents and the professional literature we have read about them have affected our classroom practices. We recognize that for adolescents, education is not the main focus. These students' family circles no longer serve as their primary community. Adolescents feel the urge to go beyond their families—to their peers. As puberty begins, the social world of adolescents takes precedence. While students have entered Piaget's formal operational stage, hockey games, phone calls, dance class, dating, and friendships compete with their motivation to learn. Middle school students crave independence—making decisions about their own lives, forming relationships with their peers, and fitting into a social circle. As students strive to be independent, they must grapple with uncertainties that affect their self-esteem. Physical, emotional, intellectual, and social changes mark this complex stage of young adulthood, and pose a challenge for educators.

Two Schools of Thought

Our research about language learning made us cognizant of theories and practices underlying two schools of thought—explicit instruction and whole language. Our research made clear that both approaches have strengths that facilitate student learning. It also became apparent that educators frequently choose only explicit instruction or only whole language as the basis of classroom instruction. Explicit instruction and whole language are often seen as polar opposites—one rigid, the other flowery—when in effect they are not.

Explicit Instruction

Explicit instruction dates back to the stereotypical one-room school house: The teacher possesses the knowledge and the students are there to receive it, write it, and recite it. Morrow and Tracey (1997) define explicit instruction as "the systematic, sequential presentation" of skills that uses "isolated, direct instructional strategies" (p. 646). Explicit, teacher-directed instruction is employed to equip students with factual knowledge of concepts and skills; however, when explicit instruction is the primary mode of instruction in a classroom, reading and writing skills are taught in isolation, usually by means of grammar books, basal readers, and worksheets. This instructional approach does not make apparent to students how these skills are used in the real world. When explicit instruction is employed without regard to the use of these skills in the world outside school, concepts and skills are isolated and meaningful learning does not occur.

Whole Language

Whole language emerged as a method of language instruction in the 1970s, as researchers including Courtney Cazden, Carol Edelsky, Yetta and Ken Goodman, and Frank Smith observed students and teachers and reflected on classroom practices. These researchers based their findings and conclusions on the works of time-honored researchers such as Piaget, Vygotsky, and Chomsky.

Yatvin (1991) explains that whole language is "the belief that language learning depends on the learner's self-confidence, and integration of real language use into learning activities" (p. 2). When whole language is the primary mode of instruction in the classroom, reading and writing skills are integrated, have real purposes, and are taught using authentic texts. Students' interests and prior knowledge are respected. Although whole language does focus on real language use and meaningful activities, it may leave gaps in skills and concepts that the experts have determined are necessary for students to achieve excellence and become productive citizens.

An Alternative Method:
A Combined Approach

Explicit instruction reigned in classrooms for hundreds of years. In the past 20 years, whole language became the accepted practice in many classrooms, and explicit instruction was taboo. Our purpose as educators of reading and writing in middle school is to enable students to become lifelong readers, writers, and learners. We believe this can be achieved by using a combined approach—one that embraces aspects of both whole language and explicit instruction and that acknowledges the unique nature of adolescence.

materials

Explicit instruction, itself, is not the problem; rather, the problem is the materials traditionally used in explicit instruction and especially their misuse. Many of these materials—grammar books, workbooks, basals—decontextualize language and simulate reading and writing. Because these materials do not engage students in meaningful communication activities or provide for student choices, explicit instruction alone does not achieve the goal of developing a community of readers and writers.

A middle school teacher must construct a classroom where students see the connection between reading and writing and view themselves as a "club" of readers who write and writers who read (Smith, 1992). Once this occurs, learning becomes meaningful. The combined approach is particularly helpful for adolescents because they respond best in the classroom when they are invested in their learning—they construct knowledge about language because it has personal meaning. The connection of reading and writing and meaningful learning together form the basis of our philosophy.

The movement toward a combined approach for teaching reading and writing begins with the teacher. First, a teacher must adopt his or her own philosophy that incorporates different theories and practices; this is accomplished by educating oneself about language learning and adolescent development through professional literature and by reflecting on one's practices. When a teacher has his or her own eclectic approach to teaching reading and writing, the transformation from only explicit instruction or only whole language to a combined approach has begun.

Once teachers have developed their own philosophy, the classroom can become an environment that supports students as they develop a love and appreciation for reading and writing. More activities emerge that practice and study language in ways that are closely related to ways students will use it in the real world—a condition adolescents value. The students and the teacher choose among contemporary works, classics, fiction, nonfiction, poetry, and picture books to create an environment that enriches students' experiences with literature. After this happens, conversations about books—book talks, literature circles, and response groups—surface that are focused by the teacher but led by the students. Daily reading and writing—freewriting, sustained silent reading (SSR), and modeling of reading and writing by the teacher—also demonstrate the combined approach.

Another visible component of the combined approach involves language instruction. Lessons focusing on language conventions and skills once were only taken from grammar books and workbooks. In the combined approach, language instruction incorporates real literature to show how authors use writing skills and language conventions. The marriage of explicit instruction and whole language makes language learning meaningful and authentic.

Final Reflection

National, state, and local standards established by experts in education are written to provide a map or guide for teachers to impart necessary concepts and skills to students. Although this knowledge is fundamental to learning, pure mastery of these standards alone will not guarantee that middle school students will be inspired to become lifelong learners—independent of parents, teachers, and the standards. It is the approach a teacher adopts that builds lifelong learners. Neither explicit instruction nor whole language alone can guarantee that students will achieve the standards and develop a love of learning. The following chapter illustrates how the combined approach meets the standards and inspires lifelong readers, writers, and learners.

CHAPTER 2

How to Inspire Lifelong Readers, Writers, and Learners

O nce we adopted the idea that our purpose as teachers of reading and writing was to enable middle school students to become lifelong readers, writers, and learners, the question of how to achieve this objective perplexed us. Many questions surfaced.

- How does a teacher construct a classroom where adolescents see the connection between reading and writing?
- How does a teacher meet national, state, and local standards and make them meaningful to students?
- How does a teacher create a literacy club—readers who write and writers who read?
- What are the elements of a reading and writing program that will most inspire students to carry a love and appreciation of reading, writing, and learning into their adult lives?

The workshops, experts, professional readings, and professors we encountered each provided small pieces of this puzzle, serving as the foundation on which our combined approach was built; however, organizing and putting the approach into practice still eluded us. We needed a recipe for success. *Standards for the English Language Arts* (IRA & NCTE, 1996) emerged as a key resource for us, becoming a map, guiding our choices, and making clear what pieces of the puzzle were essential to achieving our purpose.

We begin this chapter with our recipe for success. Our suggestions come from *Standards for the English Language Arts* (1996). This document sets out specific language goals—what students should know and be able to do in grades K to 12.

Follow This Recipe

- Connect reading, self, society, and cultures
- Expose students to literary texts from various genres
- Teach reading strategies
- Teach writing strategies
- Highlight language conventions
- Promote research and discovery
- Provide a variety of technological and informational resources
- Encourage a respect for diversity
- Recognize learners whose first language is not English
- Create literacy communities

We deem these goals essential to a balanced reading and writing classroom that fosters students' literacy growth. Each component of our recipe is explained first by stating the related standard or standards and then by sharing classroom snapshots of various approaches that engage readers and writers. These snapshots offer an overview of our reading and writing classrooms and illustrate how the practical approaches meet our goals and the standards. The approaches are discussed in greater detail in Chapters 3 and 4.

Connect Reading, Self, Society, and Cultures

1

Students read a wide range of print and nonprint texts to build an understanding of texts, of themselves, and of the cultures of the United States and the world; to acquire new information; to respond to the needs and demands of society and the workplace; and for personal fulfillment. Among these texts are fiction and nonfiction, classic and contemporary works. (p. 27)

In our classrooms our yearly reading and writing theme centers on choices. The literature we read addresses choices made by characters and the consequences of these choices—connecting the readings with self, society, and cultures of the United States and world. The students and the teacher discuss and reflect on real-life choices. For instance, the class reads *The Outsiders* (1967) by S.E. Hinton and *Gangs—Trouble on the Streets* (1995) by Marilyn Oliver. In *literature circles*—groups of students reading and discussing different books within a certain genre or theme—students read and discuss the demands that society puts on individuals' lives, compelling characters to make choices that result in positive or negative consequences. Students reflect on and write about how society forces them to make choices; this makes the literature come to life.

Literature circles are also utilized in a unit in which the class has the choice of reading a nonfiction piece covering either slavery or the U.S. Civil Rights movement. Students reflect on what they read and record their personal reactions to and feelings about what they have read in *double entry journals* in which students divide pages into two columns, writing summaries on the left and personal reflections on the right. In another unit, students have a choice of nonfiction pieces that pertain to the Holocaust. Students form literature circles to discuss the text and share their personal reactions and feelings; moreover, they are challenged to consider the various perspectives of the people involved.

Fifteen to 20 minutes a day is allotted for students to engage in *sustained silent reading*—a block of time at the beginning or end of the class period that allows students the opportunity to read their own choices for pleasure. This personal reading time and the literature circles encourage students to obtain personal fulfillment from reading, discussing, and writing about texts.

Standards for the English Language Arts asserts that students should "learn that literary texts are relevant to their own lives" (1996, p. 29). Our students recognize this. The reading connections to self, society, and cultures are evident to us through their classroom discussions and journal writing. Classroom dialogue and student writing not only provide opportunities for personal reflections, but they also enhance critical thinking and stimulate metacognitive awareness.

Expose Students to Literary Texts From Various Genres and Teach Reading Strategies

---

2
Students read a wide range of literature from many periods in many genres to build an understanding of the many dimensions (e.g., philosophical, ethical, aesthetic) of human experience. (p. 27)

3
Students apply a wide range of strategies to comprehend, interpret, evaluate, and appreciate texts. They draw on their prior experience, their interactions with other readers and writers, their knowledge of word meaning and other texts, their word identification strategies, and their understanding of textual features (e.g., sound-letter correspondence, sentence structure, context, graphics). (p. 31)

Students are exposed to literature from various genres. During the Holocaust, slavery, and Civil Rights movement literature circle units, students choose an autobiography or biography to read and then write their personal reflections in double entry journals. Some choices in the Holocaust unit are *Upstairs Room* by Johanna Reiss, *We Are Witnesses: Five Diaries of Teenagers Who Died in the Holocaust* by Jacob Boas, *Rescue: The Story of How Gentiles Saved Jews in the Holocaust* by Milton Meltzer, and *Hiding to Survive: Stories of Jewish Children Rescued From the Holocaust* by Maxine B. Rosenberg. Some choices in the slavery and Civil Rights movement units are *Escape from Slavery: The Boyhood of Frederick Douglass in His Own Words* by Michael McCurly, *Get On Board: The Story of the Underground Railroad* by Jim Haskins, *Witness to Freedom: Young People Who Fought for Civil Rights* by Belinda Rochelle, and *Warriors Don't Cry* by Melba Pattillo Beals.

Students are exposed to realistic fiction during whole-class guided instruction. Some of the books used are *The Cay* by Theodore Taylor, *Nothing But the Truth* by Avi, and *The Outsiders* by S.E. Hinton.

In an independent cross-curricular assignment, students select a book from the historical fiction genre set in either the colonial or Revolutionary War period in U.S. history. Students write a *character journal* in which they assume the role of the main character and write first-person diary entries reacting to one episode in each chapter. Novel choices include *The Witch of Blackbird Pond* by Elizabeth George Speare, *My Brother Sam Is Dead* by James and Christopher Collier, *Early Thunder* by Jean Fritz, *A Ride Into Morning: The Story of Tempe Wick* by Ann Rinaldi, *Sarah Bishop* by Scott O'Dell, and *Johnny Tremain* by Esther Forbes.

The science fiction genre is explored through literature circles in which students choose from various selections. Some titles used include *Interstellar Pig* by William Sleator; *A Wrinkle in Time* by Madeline L'Engle; *The Lion, the Witch, and the Wardrobe* by C.S. Lewis; *The Giver* by Lois Lowry; *The Black Cauldron* by Lloyd Alexander; *Doom Stone* by Paul Zindel; *The Hobbit* by J.R.R. Tolkien; and *Ella Enchanted* by Gail Carson Levine.

We complete a poetry workshop in which students recognize what poets do as they write, and students become poets themselves. Part of this workshop is a poet study in which students read collections from contemporary and classic poets. Some of the selections are *Poetry for Young People: Emily Dickinson* edited by Frances Schoonmaker Bolin, *Poetry for Young People: Robert Frost* edited by Gary D. Schmidt, *A Dream Keeper and Other Poems* by Langston Hughes (illustrated by Brian Pinkney), *Everywhere Faces Everywhere: Poems* by James Berry (illustrated by Reynold Ruffins), *Joyful Noise* by Paul Fleischman, and *Ordinary Things: Poems From a Walk in Early Spring* by Ralph Fletcher (illustrated by Walter Lyon Krudop).

This extensive classroom repertoire of literature exposes students to texts from various genres and meets district guidelines and state standards for reading and writing, but it is only one component of a balanced reading and writing classroom. It is equally important to equip students with the strategies that they will need to comprehend, interpret, make connections to, evaluate, and appreciate the written word.

In addition to double entry journals, character journals, and literature circles, we present strategies a reader can employ through *mini-lessons*—brief explicit instruction that begins a class period. For example, students research an island in cooperative learning groups while reading the novel *The Cay*, which is set on an island. When a research paper is taught, students are shown in a minilesson how to skim and scan a nonfiction text. Students now take an efferent stance as readers because this process allows them to interact with the written word differently than the aesthetic stance they adopt in literature circles. Minilessons on how to take notes and how to organize information into a written product follow.

Through literature circles, students practice several reading strategies: using context clues to get meaning for unknown words, formulating open-ended questions, making connections between text and the world, and summarizing the section read.

A reading strategy often used for various genres is K-W-L (Ogle, 1986)—students divide a page into three columns and list what they know in the first, what they want to know in the second, and what they learned in the third. K-W-L allows students to tap into prior knowledge, making the material more meaningful and encouraging them to raise questions that link new knowledge to their schemata.

Teach Writing Strategies and Highlight Language Conventions

4
Students adjust their use of spoken, written, and visual language (e.g., conventions, style, vocabulary) to communicate effectively with a variety of audiences for different purposes. (p. 33)

5
Students employ a wide range of strategies as they write and use different writing process elements to communicate with different audiences for a variety of purposes. (p. 35)

6
Students apply knowledge of language structure, language conventions (e.g., spelling and punctuation), media techniques, figurative language, and genre to create, critique, and discuss print and nonprint texts. (p. 36)

As readers who write and writers who read, students look at literature from a writer's point of view, becoming cognizant of what makes good writing. Students need opportunities to write for various audiences and purposes—for themselves, their peers, their teachers, and other audiences outside the classroom—in order to become writers themselves. Writing strategies and language conventions are both integral to communicating effectively; they can best be taught explicitly by using real literature and students' writing. Direct instruction provides a toolbox of skills that students can access at various stages of the writing process. The real literature and their own writing make language learning relevant, and therefore meaningful—a key to developing lifelong learners.

The need for various writing strategies surfaces as students are engaged in the stages of the writing process. When discussing the prewriting stage, students are presented with strategies such as storyboards, fiction maps, listing, peer conferencing, and clustering. During the drafting stage, the teacher, who is an active facilitator, conferences with students, encouraging them to reflect on what they have written. The teacher poses questions to prompt and probe the writer about the draft. This dialogue models for students a strategy that writers employ as they revise their work. Students return to this prompting and probing as they continue to draft; eventually, they internalize this strategy and using it becomes second nature.

Through minilessons during the revising stage of the writing process, we may focus on strengthening the lead to a narrative; students then return to their drafts and improve the leads. We may discuss the importance of dialogue, making writing more engaging for the reader. Students then revisit their pieces to add dialogue. The repertoire of questions that students use grows as they prompt and probe.

The editing stage can be addressed in a similar way. One lesson may focus on correct usage of words such as *their/there/they're*. Students also may brainstorm alternatives to using the word *said* in written dialogue and then return to their pieces to edit. In addition, students engage in weekly spelling workshops that focus on language rules and frequently misspelled words and homonyms, as well as their own spelling demons.

Students first revise and edit their own writing using self-revising and self-editing sheets that show what readers expect from their drafts. Then students are engaged as peer revisers and peer editors. The self-revising and self-editing components foster metacognitive growth and students' awareness of themselves as readers, writers, and learners. The interaction with peers in these stages of the writing process makes clear to students that writing is social.

Students publish their writing in various ways for numerous audiences. In our classrooms, one vehicle for students to become authors is by writing and illustrating a children's book for emergent readers—the blank book. This year-long project celebrates reading and writing by encouraging students to use what they have learned about authors to write and publish their own books.

A combined approach that embraces the best elements of explicit instruction and whole language leads to effective student writers who follow myriad writing strategies. Students recognize that the writing process is not linear but recursive.

Promote Research and Discovery and Provide a Variety of Technological and Informational Resources

7

Students conduct research on issues and interests by generating ideas and questions, and by posing problems. They gather, evaluate, and synthesize data from a variety of sources (e.g., print and nonprint texts, artifacts, people) to communicate their discoveries in ways that suit their purpose and audience. (p. 38)

8

Students use a variety of technological and informational resources (e.g., libraries, databases, computer networks, video) to gather and synthesize information and to create and communicate knowledge. (p. 39)

The ability to research issues and interpret the answers supplied by research resources is another valuable component of becoming lifelong readers, writers, and learners. We provide opportunities for students to practice gathering, evaluating, and synthesizing data as they research. Proficiency in these steps is vital to completing successful research; moreover, it is the communication of their discoveries that evinces students' understanding.

For example, students choose a Canadian province to research. They communicate their discoveries through postcards or diary entries. Students use the five themes of geography to guide their research: location, place, human interaction, movement, and region. They gather, evaluate, and synthesize information from primary and secondary sources. The students' purpose is to communicate their discoveries of the five themes to their audience—their classmates and teacher. The diary entries or postcards are unconventional ways to communicate the knowledge learned. This may also be an alternative assessment to an objective test.

In another unit students choose an endangered animal and conduct research according to what interests them about the species. The teacher provides a set of guidelines that will focus students on various research strategies. Students present their discoveries in a pizza box diorama that includes a research paper, a collage of pictures, and a list of written clues about the endangered animal. This unconventional presentation of research is also an alternative way to assess students' knowledge.

Skillful readers and writers are expected to be proficient in using technological and informational resources such as CD-ROM, the Internet, and computer word-processing applications. Students use CD-ROM and the Internet as resources when conducting research. The Internet also is used to build background or to provide enrichment for different topics in the classroom. When writing for publication, students are encouraged to draft, revise, and edit using a word-processing program. It is also useful to require students to communicate their knowledge of a topic not only through written assignments but also using videotape, audiotape, or drama.

Encourage a Respect for Diversity

9
Students develop an understanding of and respect for diversity in language use, patterns, and dialects across cultures, ethnic groups, geographic regions, and social roles. (p. 41)

In a classroom designed to create lifelong readers, writers, and learners, the choice of literature should center on understanding and respect for all people. Mindful of this goal, one text we include is *The Cay* by Theodore Taylor. The theme of this novel is prejudice, illustrated by two characters of different races, ages, and cultures who grow to rely on and respect each other. Timothy, a former slave who speaks with a Caribbean accent, and Phillip, a young American boy, grapple with their feelings about each other as they struggle to survive on a deserted island. As the novel progresses, their similarities and differences come to life for students, who begin to investigate their own prejudices and recognize how all people are interdependent.

Other units of our program that encourage a respect for diversity concern slavery, the Civil Rights movement, and the Holocaust. Students choose from various nonfiction texts that are read and discussed in literature circles. Literature circle discussions, *dialogue journals* (dialogue between student and teacher about something they have recently read), and double entry journals provide students with a forum to discuss, comment on, and analyze the social roles placed on individuals and to make connections to their own lives. These texts enable students to read about real people from various geographic regions who represent myriad ethnic and religious groups, encouraging a respect for diversity and, what is more important, encouraging respect for every person regardless of their similarities or differences.

Recognize Learners Whose First Language Is Not English

10

Students whose first language is not English make use of their first language to develop competency in the English language arts and to develop understanding of content across the curriculum. (p. 42)

We recognize students whose first language is not English and endeavor to use their first language to teach reading and writing skills. Many school districts have established English as a Second Language (ESL) programs that focus on students' first language; however, in some school districts a classroom teacher may have a student whose first language is not English but not have access to an ESL program to support his or her learning.

The following vignette shows how Teresa handled such a situation.

> I had not been trained in teaching ESL students, so when I learned that an ESL student would be in my classroom, I began to research and read about this.

I discovered that for ESL students to develop a competency for language learning, their first language and social interaction are essential.

A student from Portugal began his formal education in the United States in my classroom and was expected to read Portuguese books during SSR, share his reading in Portuguese, and compose freewriting and writing assignments in his own language. My grade partner and I placed labels in Portuguese and English around our classrooms that identified parts of the classroom, topics being studied, parts of the school, and various objects that he used daily. He received 30 minutes' reading instruction daily in English from a reading specialist, used a CD-ROM program titled *Wiggle Works Scholastic Beginning Literacy System* (1994), and worked with a language specialist who focused on his speaking.

As he gained proficiency in the English language, he read books written in English, attempted to discuss orally what he had read in English, wrote in English in a dialogue journal about what he was reading, and translated his writing assignments from Portuguese to English. He was mainstreamed into all special and academic classes. He developed his conversational English skills by socializing with the other students both in class and at recess.

Create Literacy Communities

11
Students participate as knowledgeable, reflective, creative, and critical members of a variety of literacy communities. (p. 44)

12
Students use spoken, written, and visual language to accomplish their own purposes (e.g., for learning, persuasion, and the exchange of information). (p. 45)

The literacy community of the classroom is a base to reach other literacy communities. As students collaborate in literature circles, peer revising and editing, author studies, group research, and other language activities, they begin to use language effectively and with authentic purposes in the classroom community. In addition, the children's books written by our students reach a variety of literacy communities such as the younger readers with whom they share their books in school, as well as the public library where they are displayed. Some students also have the opportunity to publish their writing online. When a variety of literacy communities are included as audiences for their literacy products, students feel that their work is meaningful and warrants thoughtful attention.

Our goal is to inspire our students to be motivated to read and write during, after, and beyond the school year. This autonomy is evident when students enter writing contests, read additional books by authors studied in class, urge their teachers to read the books they have read, and write stories and poems during their free time. Parents often share with us that their children discuss novels they are reading at home and request that their parents take them to bookstores and libraries. When students choose to read and write—and, hence, learn—for their own purposes, it is truly cause for celebration.

Final Reflection

Thoughtful teachers of reading and writing should consider the questions posed on the first page of this chapter. We posed these questions to ourselves and we found an answer—the combined approach. Workshops, professional literature, and professors influenced our teaching of reading and writing. *Standards for the English Language Arts* empowered us to organize and implement our combined approach, helping us to embrace the best elements of explicit instruction and whole language.

The next chapter introduces practical approaches for teachers to use as students are engaged in experiencing and responding to literature. Less complex approaches appear first, and those requiring more preparation follow. For each approach we provide our explanation, student definitions, student examples, and a rationale to show its value in the reading and writing classroom.

CHAPTER 3

Experiencing and Responding to Literature

Sam looks up toward the clock for the posted sign to find out if it is DEAR time or freewrite. Other students look in his direction as he shouts, "Yes!" and pulls *Harry Potter and the Sorcerer's Stone* from his school bag.

For 15 minutes, students and I read our own choices of reading material until I announce, "Boys and girls, please close your books, so we can begin the next part of language arts class."

"At the last literature circle meeting, each of you decided on roles to complete for the next meeting. Yesterday in our minilesson, we talked about foreshadowing. In the chapters you are about to read, you should be able to recognize the events that were foreshadowed in the previous chapters. If you notice foreshadowing, write it down in your literature response journal. We will be discussing this as a class after you talk in your literature circle during Thursday's meeting. If you finish your work, the chart has choices listed. If anyone needs help, just ask for it. You may move to any part of the room to read."

I circulate to check with students as they read. I conference with students to monitor comprehension—asking students to clarify their written comments, talking about what has been read so far, eliciting students' opinions about the text, posing scaffolding questions, and reading with a student to assist comprehension.

Peter raises his hand while pointing to a passage in the text. "Ms. Morretta, I am having trouble understanding this section."

"Pete, can you come over here for a conference about it so that no one else is being disturbed?" I respond.

Peter and I talk quietly about why he is confused while everyone else reads their text. Finally, Peter rejoins the rest of his classmates in reading independently. I continue to move around the classroom, looking for others who may need me.

"Mary, you had trouble last week with identifying examples of history writing elements in your text. How are you doing with that this week?" I quietly ask.

"Well, I am not up to that yet. I don't know. I think I understand it. I am not finished reading yet," replies Mary.

"Okay. I am sorry to have bothered you. Go ahead and read. When you get up to that assignment, see me so we can go over that. I just want to make sure you understand it."

Mary nods and says, "Sure. Thanks, Ms. Morretta."

Just then Sam approaches me. "Ms. Morretta, I am not the vocabulary finder, but I found a word that I don't understand. Should I show it to Mary or should I look it up? Mary is the vocabulary finder. I am the passage picker this week."

"I think you should look it up yourself then share it with the group even though you aren't the vocabulary finder. But before you do that, let's try to figure it out without the dictionary first. Do you remember how to do that?"

Sam thinks and then says, "Yeah, look at the words around it." Sam and I figure out the meaning of the word and both move on to our work.

"Okay, boys and girls, please finish up where you are in your work and come back to your seats," I announce, moving toward the front of the room. "We are going to begin the second half of language arts class." I remind the class about yesterday's topic—simple tenses. I distribute a picture book to each student, saying, "When you get a book, search for verbs that are in the present, past, and future tenses—share the verbs you find with your group."

The class works as I circulate to those who need help. The class finishes the activity, and we review their work. There are 5 minutes left in class, so I say, "You can now read these books for enjoyment."

The class ends the way it begins—reading for enjoyment. Students and books.

—Teresa

As this narrative shows, the dynamics of a middle school reading and writing classroom and the goal of developing lifelong readers are best managed by a teacher who provides choices, challenges, and opportunities for students to read, to write, and to discuss literature. Student choice is a main component of this reading and writing classroom as students enter the classroom and read their own material for 15 minutes. Students take an active role in their learning, and the teacher is a facilitator of learning.

In this classroom snapshot, Teresa approaches Mary to check her understanding of a literary device used by the author. Mary evaluates her own learning and communicates this to Teresa. As Teresa provides learning opportunities, both explicit instruction and aspects of whole language are embraced. The minilesson focuses on verb tenses through direct instruction, and utilizes real literature to show how authors need to understand tenses as they write. While school districts mandate particular reading and writing standards, the teacher teaches these skills by immersing students in real literature.

Through many years of teaching reading to middle school students, we have learned much from the work of Louise Rosenblatt, Nancie Atwell, Regie Routman, *The Pennsylvania Framework for Reading, Writing, and Talking Across the Curriculum* (Lytle & Botel, 1996), and our students. This knowledge affects our classroom practices, particularly the teaching of reading. Successful readers are identified as those who read not only the lines of a text, but "between and beyond the lines." How does a teacher organize instruction so that readers become actively engaged with literature? How does a teacher construct a learning environment that includes meaningful reading transactions?

An important lesson we have learned from the experts is that reading is a transaction—an interaction among reader, text, and author. Louise Rosenblatt identified two stances that readers take as they transact with a text: efferent and aesthetic. We interpret Rosenblatt's transactional theory as follows: When readers take an efferent stance, they are reading with the purpose of taking information, but when readers take an aesthetic stance, they are reading with the purpose of making personal connections.

This view of reading as a transaction has greatly influenced our combined approach. We realize that both the efferent and aesthetic stances have value; however, reading was traditionally experienced with students taking an efferent stance alone. The aesthetic stance was relegated to leisure reading outside the classroom. The materials used to teach were basal readers written to teach reading skills. Basals decontextualized language and the reading experience, erasing the "lived through" experience of readers and making void everything readers think, know, and feel as they read (Rosenblatt, 1984, p. 275). Our combined approach encourages students to take an aesthetic stance as they read literature; however, we explicitly teach certain reading strategies and literary devices that lead students to take an efferent stance. The approaches we discuss to engage readers to experience and respond to literature expect them to transact with the text and move between the two stances. Although we recognize that the teacher's role includes imparting reading strategies and literary devices, it cannot be seen as only this. If we focus on skills only, reading has no meaning for adolescents and they are not inspired to read. A teacher also must provide opportunities for students to make choices about the texts they read, to think critically and discuss their interpretations with others, and to make connections.

This chapter discusses elements of a balanced reading and writing classroom that embrace our combined approach to teaching reading in middle school. It offers samples of student work that illustrate each practice; students also contribute their "definitions" of these elements. A significant concern is how to manage the reading and writing classroom with the many demands placed on teachers—standards, time constraints, assemblies, diverse student needs, extracurricular activities, and other unforeseen interruptions. A sketch for a reading and writing unit is provided to illustrate how to manage some of these practices. Teachers are advised that this sketch is what works for us, in our classrooms, and with our students. What will work for you, for your classroom, and for your students can only be determined by you.

These classroom practices will help a teacher construct a classroom where students see the connection between reading and writing; meet national, state, and local standards; make these standards meaningful to students; create a literacy club; and inspire students to become lifelong readers, writers, and learners.

Practical Approaches That Engage Readers

Sustained Silent Reading (SSR)

> DEAR time is a time when you *drop everything and read* for 15 minutes. There is silence so it's very easy to fantasize about the book. When I read my Perry Mason mystery, I easily become the intelligent lawyer. DEAR time is a good idea because if you can't find the time to read at home or anywhere else, you can always read the book you've heard so much about!
>
> —Angelo, age 12

Students read and write daily. Although language arts periods can range from 45- to 90-minute blocks or can be separate reading and writing periods, a manageable way to begin creating a balanced reading and writing classroom is implementing *sustained silent reading* or DEAR time—a block of time at the beginning or end of the class period that allows students opportunities to read their own choices for pleasure. Pure enjoyment is the goal, yet there is an additional benefit. Routman (1991) explains, "Since there is no question that reading achievement is positively influenced by the amount of time spent reading books, we must provide time in school—even at the secondary level—for students to read books of their own choosing" (p. 42). This approach is modeled by the teacher; the teacher reads as well. Students not only experience literature, but come to value it because the teacher models and values the process by allotting classroom time for it. This time usually ranges from 10 to 20 minutes.

A balanced reading and writing classroom depends on a literacy-enriched environment that includes picture books, chapter books, novels, nonfiction books, magazines, newspapers, and student-published works. Students are immersed in literature in the classroom, and they can choose to bring their own literature to read during SSR.

The benefit of including this approach in your classroom is that it makes students value reading and inspires them to read on a regular basis about topics that interest them. The Commission on Adolescent Literacy of the International Reading Association reports in *Adolescent Literacy: A Position Statement* (Moore, Bean, Birdyshaw,

& Rycik, 1999) that adolescents deserve specific opportunities to schedule reading into their days because "time spent reading is related to reading success" (p. 5). SSR and providing student choice also support adolescents' need for independence. If students enjoy reading and anticipate this time, the foundation of becoming a lifelong reader has been set.

Children read their own choice of materials during sustained silent reading.

Dialogue Journals

My dialogue journal is a book that I write in about the books I read. I write to Ms. Morretta in it after I've read a good book. Sometimes I write for a long time, sometimes it's very short. Due on, Done on, Book, and Question, is the heading I put at the top of the page. I start with, "Dear Ms. Morretta," and end with, "Love, Suzie." Sometimes I write P.S. to finish something I thought of, but I don't do that often. My favorite part of having a dialogue journal is when Ms. Morretta writes back. It's usually brief, but I don't care 'cause she has 44 other students to write to. She always starts with, "Dear Suzie," and always ends with, "Love, Ms. Morretta."

—Suzie, age 12

The *dialogue journal*—a written exchange between students and the teacher about something they have read recently—is done on a weekly basis. Here students and teacher carry on a conversation over time, sharing ideas and feelings about books. This type of journal makes clear to students the power of dialogue and ensures that students' voices are heard. In addition, students may write to peers, their parents, or the school principal. Adolescents value this exchange of ideas that reinforces the social nature of reading.

The dialogue journal provides genuine conversation and communication between students and teacher about reading literature. A written dialogue with a real audience is an interactive conversation that gives students practice writing and communicating. In this scenario student and teacher are equal participants; two minds unite to bring about new understanding, ideas, and possibilities to each other. Frequently, as students learn from the teacher, the teacher also learns from them.

In our classrooms, students choose from a list of questions we borrowed from *In the Middle: Writing, Reading and Learning With Adolescents* (1987, pp. 276–280) by Nancie Atwell. Students write to the teacher responding to the literature they are reading, guided by a question they have chosen. Sample questions are as follows:

- Topic: What was this section about?
- Connection: Can you connect an event in the book to an event in your life? What happened? How are they alike? How are they different?
- Grace of language: Did the sentences flow? Were they choppy? Did you notice yourself thinking about how well a particular line worked?

(See the sample from a sixth grader's dialogue journal in Figure 1.)

Dialogue journals can be assessed by the teacher, who looks for thoughtful reflections that show students' new understanding, ideas, or questions on what they are reading by the assigned day (see the rubric for assessing dialogue journal entries in Figure 2 on page 26). Although correct spelling and grammar are not the major goals of dialogue journals, it is expected that students will practice these skills to the best of their abilities. This is an independent, weekly assignment that can be used as a part of students' homework grades. This is a manageable approach for students and teachers to respond to literature.

Figure 1
Sample Dialogue Journal Entries

9/21/99
Title - Out of the Dust
Question - Was there enough suspense?
Dear Ms. Moretta,
    I really don't think
there is enough suspence
because, all that happens
is dust storms. I like the
book but there should
be more action and
suspence. The book can get
a little boring because
she tells alot about
the piano and her hands.
What do you think?
             Your Student,
             Shannon T.

Dear Shannon,
    I think it doesn't necessarily
have lots of suspense, but it
has a lot of interesting things that
happen in her life! Most of which
we will never experience!
           ♡ Ms. M.

Dear Ms. Moretta,
    You're right! I never
really thought of it that
way. She went through
a lot of difficult times
that I didn't know were
possible! I don't think I
would like live if
I did threw fire on
my mom I guess the
book tells us how
lucky we are that we
have great families who
love & care about us! →

        Love,
        Shannon Thompson

    I am glad I provided
insight for you!
        ♡ Ms. Moretta

Figure 2
Rubric for Assessing Dialogue Journal Entries

1	2	3
Demonstrates an attempt to respond to text but reflections are disjointed, incomplete, or irrelevant; gives few examples from text to support reflections	Makes connections and reflections about text that show literal comprehension; gives some examples from text to support reflections	Demonstrates a thorough understanding of text through detailed, sophisticated reflections; gives many examples from text to support reflections

Double Entry Journals

> Double entry journals are great to me. I pick a statement from a book, and I express what I feel about it. It helps me enjoy the book better, and it helps me to be a better writer in my own way!!
>
> —Susan, age 12

> Double entry journals are a favor to yourself to help remember important or interesting facts in a novel or story.
>
> —Chrissy, age 12

A *double entry journal* is a journal in which students divide their page into two columns, writing summaries on the left and personal reflections on the right (see the example in Figure 3). Lytle and Botel (1996) describe such journals as a means to get students to read not just the lines of the text, but to read "between and beyond the lines" (p. 23). These journals provide a tangible sign that students are experiencing and responding to literature by taking an aesthetic stance in analyzing the text, connecting the text to their own lives, noticing similarities with other texts, questioning characters' motives, or identifying with characters.

When adults read books, they naturally connect with the book for many reasons; for example, they relate the plot to their lives or empathize with characters. The students' entries show that students can

Figure 3
Example From a Double Entry Journal

An entry about Allen Say's *Grandfather's Journey:*

Facts	Feelings
Grandfather reminisces on his childhood in Japan and his adult life in the United States. He loves Japan and America for many reasons. Grandfather is happy that he is a part of both countries. His grandson thinks about his grandfather's life and his appreciation for both cultures.	I know that my grandpop came from Poland, but I never really talked to him about it. Maybe I'll ask him next time I see him. I wonder if he had to choose one country over the other which would he choose.

make these same connections, which are beneficial to their developing into lifelong readers and strengthening their comprehension—another important goal of reading education.

Teachers may want to prompt students to think critically about and take an aesthetic stance toward the text. A list of reader-response questions are provided in Appendix A. The teacher should first model this approach to make the objectives and expectations clear.

In our reading and writing program, double entry journals are integrated early in the school year in the whole-class guided reading of *The Outsiders* by S.E. Hinton (see Figure 4 on the next page). Students reflect on prominent passages from the novel. In the example in Figure 4, comprehension as well as interaction with the text are demonstrated, showing that the reader has connected to the text "beyond the lines of the text" (Lytle & Botel, 1996, p. 23).

The double entry journal also may be used in a less guided fashion. During the slavery and Civil Rights movement units, students keep a double entry journal throughout their reading (see Figure 5 on page 29). As the example in Figure 5 demonstrates, the teacher can judge whether students have comprehended the text. A test may afford the same information about students' comprehension, but double entry

Figure 4
The Outsiders Double Entry Journal

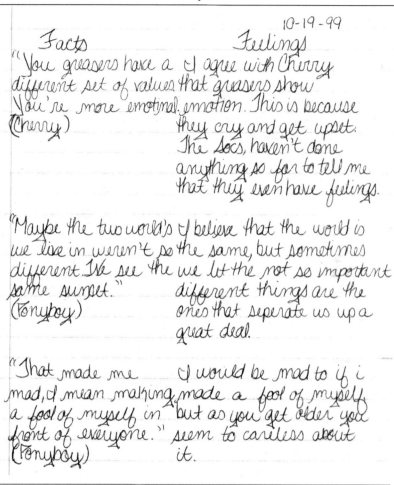

10-19-99

Facts	Feelings
"You greasers have a different set of values. You're more emotinal. (Cherry)	I agree with Cherry that greasers show emotion. This is because they cry and get upset. The Socs, haven't done anything so far to tell me that they even have feelings.
"Maybe the two world's we live in weren't so different. We see the same sunset." (Ponyboy)	I believe that the world is the same, but sometimes we let the not so important different things are the ones that seperate us up a great deal.
"That made me mad, I mean making a fool of myself in front of everyone." (Ponyboy)	I would be mad to if i made a fool of myself but as you get older you seem to careless about it.

journals do more than merely assess comprehension by encouraging students to interact with the text. These journals tap students' cognitive, affective, and social domains, thus helping to develop the whole child. The journals not only monitor students' comprehension of text, but they also initiate discussion of the text during literature circles. As seen in Figures 4 and 5, students reveal comments that demonstrate that they have become part of the text. Sometimes, it is

Figure 5
Slavery and Civil Rights Movement
Double Entry Journal

2/11/98   18

Fact	Feeling
Had to live with ar new family the Aulds Frederick had to take care of a little white boy	I think it is unfair for a boy so ung to be sold. It's wierd that Fred had to take care of a white boy I thought that was for older people. I thought it was nice
Mrs. Auld toot Fredrick the A.B.C and to spell	
Mr. Auld band Mrs. Aol from teaching Fredrick how to read.	of Mrs. Auld to try and teach Fred anything. Mr Auld is
Fredrick lean how to read from nice white boys on the street.	so much more preguice to Fred at first. Then she
Blaks rank with animals back then.	just truned mean on Fred. I think
Your responses are thoughtful. You did a nice job! ❤	it was nice of thows white boys to teach Fred how to read. It's just plan old rude to rank blanks with the animals

29

evident that students are frustrated, outraged, saddened, or excited by the author's words. This is truly an example of adolescents experiencing as well as responding to literature while engaged in meaningful activity, which fosters their motivation to read.

Because these entries are completed while students read and because they reflect students' meaning-making processes as they read, double entry journals are not graded as a traditional essay, book report, or other writing assignment. These journals are not published pieces that are revised and edited and should not be graded as such. Double entry journals reflect students' metacognition; students construct meaning of texts as they read. Although double entry journals are not graded traditionally, we expect thoughtful reflections on what is being read. The entries can be assessed for the extent of students' comprehension—disjointed, literal, extending beyond the text, or elaborated and sophisticated. We use a rubric similar to the one in Figure 6 to assess students' comprehension. The individual teacher can decide how to use this assessment in students' evaluations or report cards.

Figure 6
Rubric for Assessment of Student Comprehension

1	2
Demonstrates an attempt to respond to text but reflections are disjointed, incomplete, or irrelevant	Makes connections/reflections about text, but they are not integral to the text; literal comprehension

3	4
Makes connections to personal experiences, other texts, and/or background knowledge; is reflective in the interpretation of the text; elaborates and extends comprehension beyond the text	Demonstrates a thorough understanding of the text through detailed elaboration and extensions of text with sophisticated ideas, insights, and reflections

Reading/Writing Workshop

Reading and Writing Workshop
is a lot of fun
it makes us sad when we are done

Mini lessons do come first
Learning English makes us burst
Then we break up into stations
To work on all our situations

One station we can't talk at all
But reading there you'll have a ball
You can write poems there
Sometimes silence is hard to bear

One place you read in pairs of two
Just someone else and you

Like we said it's lots of fun
And we're sad when it is done

—Anthony, age 12, and Ian, age 12

Adolescents, like adults, want to choose what they read and write; therefore, teachers need to create a reading and writing environment that encourages choice, and they need to provide classroom time for reading and writing. In our classrooms we meet these needs through *reading/writing workshop*—time allotted for students to choose to read, write, or work on their reading and writing portfolios. Atwell's book *In the Middle* discusses reading workshop and writing workshop, as separate; we combine her ideas into one workshop. The idea of reading/writing workshop shows students that we value reading and writing as a whole, and not just as a collection of skills.

Reading/writing workshop occurs once a week. It is a 75- to 90-minute block of time. We begin with a *minilesson*—a period of brief explicit instruction. Atwell (1987) refers to a minilesson as "a brief meeting that begins the workshop where the whole class addresses an issue that's arisen in previous workshops or in pieces of students' writing" (p. 77). The teacher spends anywhere from 15 to 30 minutes on a topic that is not covered during weekly lessons. Minilessons can cover anything from managerial topics to direct instruction. Some typical minilessons may include reviewing the different stations of the workshop and the expectations in each, and modeling effective methods for peer revising and editing.

There are certain rules for reading/writing workshop. All students must read, write, or work on portfolios. Completing homework or other course work is not permitted, and this is not a study period. Students are able to move around the room freely, using whatever supplies are needed. They are allowed to lie on the floor on pillows, and they can recline on comfortable furniture such as benches or sofas.

Students may choose to work in any of three stations, depending on what reading or writing they have chosen to do. The station definitions are placed on a chart and are visible during weekly workshop; signs are posted at each station as well. Students who do not abide by the rules of reading/writing workshop lose their privileges and return to their seats to complete their work independently.

No Man's Land—This is an area away from the rest of the class. There is complete silence here for those who wish to read or write. Pillows and a large rug are provided.

Conference Station—This is where students can meet with peers to revise and edit writing or read together for enjoyment. Rugs are provided at this station if possible.

Central Reading/Writing Station—This is a center where students can work next to but not necessarily with someone. Minimal talking occurs here. This center is usually where the students' desks are located.

During reading/writing workshop a choice available to students is the blank book, which each student works on as a year-long writing assignment for eventual publication. Other choices are to write for a book report, poetry contest, or writing contest; grade poetry books; read one's own material; freewrite; or work on portfolios.

Literature Circles

All of the week,
You read a book and seek,
knowledge on a certain topic.

You fill out a sheet,
And then you meet,
with the people that are in your group.

You talk about your book,
As Ms. Morretta goes around to look,
to see how we are doing.

To me, it's good,
I think other teachers should,
do what we are doing.

—Mike, age 12

According to Owens (1995), *literature circles* are "discussion groups in which children meet regularly to talk about books" (p. 2). The fundamental value of literature circles is that they encourage students to search for meaning in a text, to build on their own comprehension, and to expand it to include the varied interpretations of others. The meaning students make from the text is elaborated on by the insight of others. Students are given opportunities to reconcile their own interpretations of the text with those of other literature circle members, fostering critical thinking. Wilhelm (1997) states this idea more succinctly, "Reading, instead of a complex set of skills, becomes a social practice and a search for meaning" (p. 17). Adolescents highly value the social aspect of their lives, so classroom practices that are social motivate students to be engaged in their learning.

Because critical thinking is the purpose of literature circles, assessment is secondary. Students are accountable for completing weekly assignments and being active participants in the discussions. They are assessed on the basis of whether they are active participants. The teacher circulates among the groups and observes students' participation in the literature circle meetings. The teacher takes a less visible role in guiding the reading instruction during literature circles, although frequently he or she becomes a participant in the discussion. Using the Teacher Reflection Sheet (see Appendix B), the teacher compiles anecdotal records for each student, noting the following behaviors: asking questions thoughtfully, listening actively to others, responding thoughtfully to others, making predictions, retelling the story, responding to the author's craft of writing, using the text to support ideas or opinions, responding to the elements of literature, completing role assignments, reflecting on reading, and cooperating with the group.

Students also reflect on their participation in the literature circle using the Literature Circle Evaluation: Cooperative Learning Reflection Sheet (see Appendix C). They evaluate themselves as participants, focusing on the extent of their participation and the quality of their contribution. In addition, they evaluate the group dynamics, focusing on the strategies used at the literature circle meeting. Students decide which strategies were successful and which were not: listening carefully, contributing appropriate information, staying on topic, maintaining eye contact, being considerate of others' opinions, and using appropriate voice levels. They then set goals for themselves and for the group for the next literature circle meeting. Both reflective assessment tools may be utilized by the individual teacher.

Teachers use literature circles to promote discussion of the text and to teach local, state, and national reading and writing standards. Literature circles may be implemented in a variety of ways, one of which is guided reading, in which the whole class reads one book. The teacher divides the book into sections; each section is the reading assignment for the week. Students are placed in cooperative learning groups, reading for 3 days and meeting for discussion on the fourth day. Before students begin to read the text, the teacher introduces a reading strategy to help readers construct meaning or teaches a literary device used by the author. For each section of the book, students focus their discussion on these minilessons.

A more student-directed way to implement literature circles involves groups of students reading different books within a certain genre or theme. When students choose from a list of books within a genre or theme, the literature circle groups are determined by students' choices of four or five texts. The novels are divided into sections, and each student performs a certain role. The role assignment sheets (see Appendixes D, E, F, and G) we use were adapted from Harvey Daniels's *Literature Circles: Voice and Choice in Student-Centered Classrooms* (1994). We have modified and implemented the following roles in our classrooms: *discussion director*—formulates open-ended questions as well as directing the discussion; *connector*—notes connections between the text and the outside world; *passage picker/summarizer*—chooses key passages to share with the group and also summarizes the text; and *word finder*—finds new and important words. During this type of literature circle, students construct knowledge by completing the assigned roles and then performing them in a discussion format at the weekly literature circle meeting. These role assignment sheets are used as a springboard to elicit thoughtful conversation that shows reading beyond the author's words—another tangible sign that students are experiencing and responding to literature. Appendixes H, I, J, and K offer sample lesson plans for literature circles for whole-class reading of a fiction text, a student-selected text within the science fiction genre, a student-selected text within the nonfiction genre, and a student-selected text within the nonfiction genre, using double entry journals.

Literature circles propel students from solely literal comprehension of text to critical thinking about the text. In a literature circle, students are engaged with the text, sitting with peers, raising questions, and co-constructing meaning through discussion. Literature circles are implemented primarily because they promote this discussion and students analyze texts in valuable and natural ways that foster the growth of lifelong readers. According to Rosenblatt (1978), educators are responsible for helping students to employ both the efferent and aesthetic stances when transacting with a text. Literature circles succeed in imparting the reading skills (efferent stance) mandated by state and local standards; moreover, they encourage students' personal interaction (aesthetic stance) with the text. The discussions that emerge during literature circle meetings are tangible signs that students are experiencing and responding to literature.

In literature circles students are engaged with the text and each other, co-constructing meaning through discussion.

How to Manage Practical Approaches That Engage Readers

Essential to the growth of a community of readers and writers is how teachers manage reading and writing classrooms. Primarily, students must be cognizant of how the room works. Teachers should make known their expectations and students' responsibilities during SSR, when responding in dialogue journals or double entry journals, and while running and participating in literature circle discussions. When expectations are clear, the classroom is one of pure enjoyment for students and teachers. Students now view themselves as participants in learning—co-constructors—not receivers of information. Students view teachers as participants and facilitators of learning, as well as co-constructors.

A sketch of a typical week using a 75-minute block is provided in Figure 7 to demonstrate how a teacher can manage the reading and writing classroom. This sketch can be modified for those reading and writing classrooms that range from 45- to 90-minute blocks. In the

Figure 7
Schedule of Typical Week

Monday

SSR 15 minutes

Students read and write in their double entry journals that will be discussed on Friday before reading/writing workshop.

Reading of Text 30 minutes

Minilesson: Context clues

Explain the schedule—independent or paired reading of assigned pages and completion of role assignments. Remind students of other choices if work is completed before weekly meeting. Chart lists other choices: Web sites for research, work on book talk of your text, work on book report, read another literature circle book or other material, or work on your portfolio.

Students move to read. Teacher meets with students who need direct instruction in reading, pair reads with students having trouble, and answers questions about the text they are reading.

Writing Instruction 30 minutes

Introduce verb tenses as a way the writer tells the reader the timeframe an action or state of being happens in the book without reference to a clock: the way the writer conveys time to the reader. Chart examples of simple tenses. Use *Alexander and the Terrible, Horrible, No Good, Very Bad Day* by Judith Viorst to show past tense and *Stellaluna* by Janelle Cannon to show future tense. Use overheads of certain pages. Discuss what tenses the writer used. Close with notes about verb tenses to be recorded in the students' daily writing journals.

Tuesday/Wednesday

Freewrite 15 minutes

Reading of Text 30 minutes

Remind students of responsibilities and expectations. Students move to any place in the classroom to read the text pages that they have decided on as a literature group at last meeting.

No minilesson is necessary on these days. Teacher continues to meet with students who need direct instruction in reading. As students begin to complete assigned reading and roles, they show the teacher their work and then move to the "other choices" chart. This is also time for the teacher to check work for comprehension, redirect students, and clarify what is unclear. Individual attention is possible for students who need it.

Writing Instruction 30 minutes

Tuesday: Continue the lesson from Monday. Have students go to either their own writing or picture books to find examples of each simple tense as a group.

Wednesday: Create a word collage of simple tenses. If isolated skill practice of verb tenses is needed, give example sentences from students' literature circle books. Students underline the verbs and tell the tense of each.

Thursday

SSR 15 minutes

Literature Circle Meeting 30 minutes

Students run the literature circle meeting, completing their assigned role. Discussion director is in charge of the circle. Teacher circulates, making anecdotal records. When the discussion is completed, students select pages of text and choose role assignments for the next meeting. Students are set for next Monday. They complete their cooperative reflection/evaluation sheet of the literature circle.

Spelling Workshop 30 minutes

Work on biweekly words that are taken from a most-confused-words list, words from across the curriculum, a most frequently misspelled words list for the grade level, their own writing words, and words that follow the basic spelling rules. Work in groups doing various activities with the lists, depending on the focus.

Spelling workshop is explained in more detail in the next chapter.

Friday

Literature circle members discuss SSR reading, using double entry journals. **15 minutes**

Reading/Writing Workshop

Students update their reading and writing logs, writing down what they have been reading and writing all week.

Minilesson 30 minutes

Focus on using the same verb tense throughout a piece of writing. Show how writers are consistent with verb tense by reading aloud a passage from a literature circle text. Show a student's book report on the overhead, checking for consistent use of verb tense. In small groups, students edit the writing piece, making the verb tenses consistent. Share results.

Stations 30 minutes

Students choose to read, write, or work on their portfolios. Teacher confers with students about their writing or reteaches language skills to students who need more practice.

Choices for the students are blank book, writing poems, reading of any material, working on portfolio for conferences, writing and poetry contests, or book reports.

45-minute block, the reading minilesson would remain, but the reading of the text would be assigned to be completed outside class. The literature circle meeting would remain either on Thursday or as a component of reading/writing workshop on Friday. In the 90-minute block, the teacher can include both freewriting and SSR. The individual classroom teacher is aware of what standards must be met, the school's schedule, and practices that the teacher would like to include. Each teacher can modify the schedule provided to match the demands of the standards to be met, the school's schedule, and individual teacher preferences.

Final Reflection

A balance of explicit instruction and whole language creates a dynamic, student-centered middle school classroom that leads to the development of a community of readers and writers. Using real literature to teach language skills is crucial and fundamental to reaching this goal; moreover, students need to experience and to respond to literature through various approaches.

It is precisely how students experience and respond to literature that shapes this developing community of readers and writers. The approaches that teachers practice determine the success of this community. Teachers who communicate that they value reading and writing and their students' responses to it witness the growth of a thriving learning environment. When classroom activities afford time, choice, and opportunities for reading, writing, and talking about literature, adolescents come to value reading and writing. Students begin to look forward to opportunities to express themselves in writing in dialogue journals and double entry journals, and to express themselves by speaking in literature circle discussions and cooperative learning groups. Reading and writing are meshed into students' daily lives; students even begin to make time outside the classroom to read, write, and talk about books. The classroom supports students' development as readers and writers, and it fortifies their identification as readers and writers.

The next chapter introduces practical approaches for teachers to utilize as students are engaged in writing for an audience. The approaches discussed—freewriting, minilessons, conferencing and assessment, spelling workshop, and reading/writing workshop (high-lighting publishing student work)—are essential elements of writing instruction. Again student definitions complement our explanations, and rationales are included to show the value of these approaches in the reading and writing classroom.

CHAPTER 4

Writing for Readers

As Bob entered my classroom, I noticed him clutching his story-board for his pet rock story. During the 10-minute freewriting at the beginning of class, Bob wrote furiously in his daily writing journal. In my freewriting, I noted that yesterday Bob had complained of writer's block when I introduced the storyboard; however, today that wasn't a problem. During our sharing of freewriting, Bob did not volunteer to read his freewriting to the class. I was disappointed because I was curious about what had made him write so ferociously. I would soon find out.

After our literature discussion groups for *The Outsiders*, some of my students continued to plan their stories using their story-boards, and others were beginning their first drafts. Bob looked at Jim's storyboard and was questioning him when I approached their table for a conference.

"Ms. Ambrosini, what do you think of his storyboard? Isn't it phat? Doesn't Rocke look cool?" Bob remarked as he held up Jim's storyboard.

"Bob's is good too." Jim announced. "I knew Bob's story was going to be scary because he's always reading R.L. Stine. Even his blank book is scary. I saw his fiction map during reading/writing workshop. It's about two friends who are chased by a ghost that lives at their grandmother's house," Jim commented before I could respond.

"Jim's storyboard does show Rocke's adventure. I like the details—the snake pit, the quicksand, and Rocke falling over the waterfall." I indicated. "Bob, I can tell your narrative is going to be very adventurous, too. It is obvious you have put your rock in danger. Your sketches show your rock's courage. What's going to happen after he falls off the cliff?"

"I don't know yet, but during freewriting I was thinking about using this." Bob opened to the paragraph he had written at the beginning of class. "What do you think?"

After reading it, I inquired, "What do you like about it?"

"I used some good action words—like *snatched*, *barreling*, and *bolted*." Bob pointed out. "And I'm going to be the one who saves him from the vampire."

"I like those words, too. How does the vampire enter the scene? What is your character going to do to save the day?"

"I know!" Jim, who had already begun his first draft, interrupted. "He can have the rock fall off a cliff near a haunted house where the vampire lives. Bob, you can be there with your friends who dare you to enter it."

"I think I'll make it a cave. Remember when we went to Carlsbad Caverns last year? It looked like it could be haunted. It was dark, hot, and smelled like licorice. I'll still save him though." Bob confirmed as he continued to sketch his storyboard.

Jim nodded in agreement as he continued writing. "I know where I'm using my ellipsis. Right after Rocke falls from the waterfall. You won't know if he lives or dies." Jim explained as he handed me the draft. "It'll keep you wondering just like S.E. Hinton did in *The Outsiders* when the Socs rumble with the Greasers."

"This does build suspense." I confirmed as I read Jim's draft. "Rocke's conflicts with the snake and the quicksand are described very well. You've really shown me what is happening and how Rocke responds to the danger. This line—'Rocke used his bandanna to wipe the sweat that dripped down his beet red face'—shows me Rocke's fear and fatigue. What about during the waterfall? You mention Rocke feels scared, but your words don't show me that. Try to revise that. See if you have a showing sentence you could use on the list the class made during our minilesson on showing not telling."

"Could I make up my own?" Jim wondered.

"Sure. No problem. Maybe the list will inspire you," I responded.

Inspired is how I felt as I walked to the next group to conference. They're authors, I thought. They have begun to talk like authors, to respond like authors, and to connect reading and writing like authors do.

—Michelle

As this narrative shows, the dynamics of a middle school reading and writing classroom and the goal of developing lifelong writers are best managed by a teacher who provides choices, challenges, and opportunities for students to read, to write, and to discuss. The young adults again make choices, take an active role in their learning, consult with the teacher-facilitator, and now are cognizant that they are writing for readers.

In this classroom snapshot, Michelle moves from student to student. The recursive nature of the writing process is evident as Bob and Jim refer to Bob's storyboard while drafting and then begin to conference with one another about the previous day's minilesson—showing, not telling. Michelle recognizes her role as a facilitator by prompting the boys to continue their conference. In addition, Bob and Jim connect writing to reading as they note the influence of R.L. Stine and S.E. Hinton on their writing styles—an awareness of writing for an audience. School districts mandate specific reading and writing standards, but the teacher teaches these skills in a way that makes them meaningful to the student writers.

Through many years of teaching writing to middle school students, we have learned much from our students and from professional literature by Frank Smith, Donald Graves, and Nancie Atwell, as well as others. This knowledge affects our classroom practices, particularly the teaching of writing. Experts have identified the characteristics of effective writing—focus, content, organization, style, and conventions—but how does a teacher impart these characteristics to students? How does a teacher make English grammar—direct objects, predicate nouns, infinitives, future progressive verb tense—meaningful to students?

A significant lesson we have learned from the experts is that process writing affords students the choices, time, and structure that are essential for developing effective writers. The writing process has been presented as having five distinct stages: prewriting, drafting, revising, editing, and publishing; however, although these stages provide structure for teachers and students, they are recursive, not linear. Donald Graves (1994) warns teachers about this misunderstanding of the writing process: "Of course, these processes do exist, but each child uses them differently. We simply cannot legislate their precise timing" (p. 82). This recursive view of the writing process has informed our combined approach to teaching writing.

Students revise their own drafts.

The stages of the writing process are taught and practiced. We begin by offering choices within each stage. For example, prewriting may appear as a storyboard, a fiction map, clustering, listing, or discussion. Once students have a working knowledge of the stages and the various options within them, they then begin to use them as they write. Students write frequently in our classrooms—daily freewriting, journal writing, informational writing, poetic writing, and guided writing (topics may be student selected or district requirements)—while the teacher conferences with and responds to writers as they move among the stages of the writing process. Thus, the students see themselves as writers, know themselves as writers, recognizing their strengths and weaknesses, and make choices about using the writing process.

The teacher's role has a definite impact on students as they move through the writing process. The teacher is not only teaching, but is now a facilitator, moving in and out of conferences with students with an awareness of their needs. For example, the teacher may conference with one student about the lack of organization in a draft that is confusing to the reader. The teacher and student return to the storyboard (prewriting) to revise the piece for organization. With another student, the teacher may conference about a section that fails to provide images for the reader. The teacher directs the student to a minilesson that illustrates how dialogue can be used to paint a picture for the reader. The teacher is immersed in the dynamics of students' writing at different stages of the writing process for different students.

In the real world no one is quizzed on the qualities of effective writing or asked to find the direct object in a sentence. However, a person is expected to communicate effectively in writing and in speaking. Simply explaining this to adolescents is not enough. A teacher's job is to make language learning meaningful to students and lead them to be invested in their writing. Process writing affords this through the revising and editing stages using minilessons that focus on language conventions and writing strategies that equip the writer with the skills and strategies needed to communicate effectively as they write for readers.

This chapter continues the discussion of the elements of a combined approach to language arts instruction. Sample student work illustrates each practice and students offer their definitions of them. These classroom practices will help a teacher construct a classroom where adolescents see the connection between reading and writing; where students' knowledge meets national, state, and local standards; and where these standards become meaningful to students, ultimately creating a community of students who are inspired to become lifelong readers, writers, and learners.

Practical Approaches That Engage Writers

Freewriting

> Before we really begin learning in class each morning, we have a freewrite. This enables students to write down in their own words what they are feeling, ideas they have, etc., and what they are thinking that day. Now that I think of it, we are really learning when we have freewrite. We are learning about ourselves and our writing. Freewrite can launch new short stories or blank book ideas. It definitely helps me a lot.
>
> —Elizabeth, age 12

Students read and write on a daily basis. One manageable way to commence creating a balanced reading and writing classroom is implementing *freewriting*—a block of time at the beginning or end of the class period that allows students opportunities to write about topics of their choice. This approach is modeled by the teacher, who also writes and then shares with the class, prompting students to share their freewriting. Although there are many facets to what constitutes "good writing," the sharing of freewriting affords the teacher the opportunity to highlight some of these facets: creating images, demonstrating particular writing styles, or exhibiting strong voices. Students become less inhibited and more comfortable with writing and with sharing their writing. This is the foundation for becoming a community of writers.

The benefit of including freewriting in your classroom is that students become writers, readers, and listeners. Students are inspired and motivated to write more regularly, and they anticipate an authentic purpose—the community of writers is their real audience. Students feel comfortable with writing; the groundwork of becoming lifelong writers has been established.

Students freewrite about topics of their choice.

Minilessons to Teach Writing

> Minilessons helped me to improve my writing in various ways. When writing after a minilesson, I made sure to remember everything I was taught in that lesson and in previous lessons. They also gave me new ways to revise and edit my writing by myself. For instance, the minilesson "Said Is Dead" taught me to broaden my vocabulary. I used to always write "She said" and "He said." Now, I use words such as *pronounced, announced, exclaimed,* and *proclaimed.* This makes my writing much more interesting. Minilessons give students small tricks to use in their writing and make it more enjoyable for both the reader and the writer.
>
> —Gen, age 12

Both writing strategies and language conventions are integral to readers' effective written communication. These strategies and conventions can best be taught through explicit instruction using real literature and students' writing—the combined approach. Minilessons within the combined approach provide a toolbox of skills that adolescents can access at various stages of the writing process. *Adolescent Literacy: A Position Statement* (Moore, Bean, Birdyshaw, & Rycik, 1999) states that "expert teachers help students get to the next level of strategy development by addressing meaningful topics, making visible certain strategies, then gradually releasing responsibility for the strategies to the learners" (p. 7).

The transition from isolated grammar activities to minilessons that utilize real literature and students' writing demonstrates that it is authors—students or published—who best "teach" language skills. These minilessons make language learning meaningful because they show *why* students as authors need these skills—giving them an authentic purpose for language learning, the key to motivating adolescents.

Three types of minilessons have emerged from our classroom experiences. Some minilessons that surface during the editing stage address language conventions focusing on skills to improve the mechanics of a written piece. For example, we investigate run-on sentences. We read an unedited student example to show that run-on sentences make writing difficult to read. By experiencing the difficulty in comprehending a text plagued with run-ons, students see the benefit of the lesson—making language learning meaningful.

Another type of minilesson deals with writing strategies that encourage revising for focus, content, organization, and style. For example, we discuss *leads*—typical (boring) leads versus engaging leads—when teaching how to strengthen the beginning of a writing piece to better involve the reader. This minilesson encourages students to take a second look at their writing—adding, deleting, or rearranging parts of it. The various types of engaging leads are taught explicitly, making students aware of them. Meaningful language learning occurs when students return to their writing pieces and reconstruct their leads to engage readers. Students are invested in their writing, so they want to engage readers.

The final type of minilesson may not affect writing visibly, yet it provides students with information on how our English language works. It is important for a teacher to explain to students why knowledge of the English language is valuable to them and for them to understand that there are different audiences for their writing and their speaking. Writing and speaking for peers is different than writing and speaking for those outside one's peer group. A conversation among friends differs from a conversation between a person and a prospective employer. A friendly letter is different from a business letter. These differences must be highlighted for students, which again makes language learning meaningful.

Minilessons that address these concerns show that proper usage is necessary to communicate in the real world. For example, we teach that linking verbs take predicate nouns whereas actions verbs take direct objects. At first, this seems irrelevant to the real world of the student. The teacher's job is to expand students' understanding of the English language so they recognize that this is the foundation for correct pronoun usage in speaking and in writing. A teacher can now present subject and object pronouns and show how they are used. Subject pronouns follow linking verbs; object pronouns follow action verbs. It becomes clear to students that both lessons are necessary to communicate in the real world, especially in speech.

The following minilessons are examples from our classrooms. Middle school students, by nature, need relevant reasons to become invested in learning. Teachers need to make learning meaningful by using real authors and students' writing to teach language.

Sample Minilessons Within the Combined Approach

Type #1: Language conventions that can improve the mechanics of a written piece.

Objective: To know when and how to use possessive nouns in writing.

Procedure:
1. Ask students to show how they would explain in writing that there is more than one boy or girl in the classroom. Record responses, showing that plural nouns indicate quantity, not ownership.

2. Ask students to choose an object in the classroom and show in writing that it belongs to the teacher. Record responses, noting the use of singular possessive nouns.

3. Ask students to show in writing that a particular object belongs to the boys in the classroom. Record responses, noting the use of most plural possessive nouns.

4. Ask students to record the rules that they have come to understand in this discussion.
   - Plural nouns—tell how many—add *s* or *es* to most words
   - Possessive nouns—show ownership

     singular possessive noun—add *'s* as in "Mary's book"

     most plural possessive noun—add *s'* as in "boys' hockey sticks"

5. Have students read the short story "A Creature of Habit" by Ambrose Bierce in small groups. They are to highlight any possessive nouns in the story and note whether they are singular or plural.

6. Teacher and students review the story aloud.

7. Various follow-up activities:
   - Find possessive nouns in the newspaper; indicate if singular or plural.
   - Teacher shows an example of a student book report (with student's permission) that has errors in usage of possessive nouns. In small groups, students edit the writing to correct the errors.

- Each student interviews a classmate about his or her likes or dislikes. The student writes a paragraph that includes possessive nouns.

Type #2: Writing strategies that encourage revising for focus, content, organization, or style.

Objective: To revise writing to include a lead that engages a reader.

Procedure:
1. Teacher presents and discusses different kinds of leads that are displayed on an overhead transparency.

Writing Leads

Typical (boring) lead:

It was the summer of 1999. My whole family was on vacation at the Jersey Shore. We went to the beach with all our stuff. My sister started yelling near the water.

Action lead (a character doing something):

As we trudged along the hot sand, I could see the waves crashing and the seagulls swooping in the blue sky. This peaceful scene quickly changed as my sister frantically screamed and pointed toward the ocean. I dropped my beach towel, kicked off my flip flops, and raced toward her.

"Shark!" she hollered.

Dialogue lead (a character saying something):

"Shark!" my sister hollered. "Mike, get over here. Hurry! Come on!"

"I'm coming as fast as I can." I dropped my beach towel, flung my flip flops, and raced toward my sister Janey.

Reaction lead (a character thinking about something):

I couldn't imagine what Janey was freaking out about now. All I wanted to do was come to the beach and ride my boogie board. But no, Janey's hysterics interrupted my plans. What could she be yelling about now? Yesterday she screamed when she stepped into seaweed. The day before that, she was bothered by the swooping seagulls. Today—who knows?

"Shark!" she screamed, shazattering my thoughts.

Descriptive lead:

As I trudged along the hot sand that burnt my feet, I noticed the waves crashing and the seagulls swooping in the blue sky. Arguing seagulls and laughing swimmers as well as the scent of coconut suntan lotion welcomed me back. This inviting setting quickly changed as my sister frantically screamed and pointed toward the ocean, shattering my thoughts like breaking glass.

Question lead:

What could Janey be yelling about now? Doesn't she realize that she looks ridiculous—screaming and pointing at the water's edge?

2. Have students independently search their freewriting for typical, boring leads that could be revised.

3. Have students share their boring leads in small groups. The group decides on one of the leads to be revised. The teacher assigns the group a type of lead to use in its revision. The group copies the improved lead onto chart paper to share with the whole class.

Type #3: Information on how the English language works.

Objective: To use *lie* and *lay* correctly.

Procedure:

1. Give the correct form of the verbs *lie* and *lay* on chart paper.

2. Encourage a class discussion about the confusion and irregularity of the two verbs.

3. Using the short story "A Creature of Habit," point out examples of how both verbs are used. Students discuss as a group the differences between the two verbs in order to be able to explain them.

> Dr. Spier grabbed the corpse by the arms and *laid* it on its back.
> • to place or put (*lay, laid, laid/laying*)
>
> But if you place it on its back, it will *lie* quickly.
> • to rest horizontally; reclining (*lie, lay, lain/lying*)

4. Discuss with students that the past tense of *lie* is *lay*, which causes confusion. This language rule needs students' careful attention in speaking and writing. Students need to consider

verb tense as well as correct usage when using either *lie* or *lay* in speaking and writing.

5. Two volunteers act out the example sentences, showing the obvious difference in meaning and usage.

6. Students in pairs write sentences using both verbs and act them out for the class.

Conferencing

> Conferencing is a way to help me correct my work and make it better. Through conferences I learned how to improve my work. I got the help I needed to revise my work.
>
> —Ellen, age 12
>
> Conferencing is a time where we meet with the teacher and share our writing. Conferencing was always very helpful because I could get someone else's honest opinion about my writing. I always felt that my writing was better after I conferenced because I would always get help from my teacher on how to improve what I wrote. It also helped because once we've read our writing out loud to the teacher we can hear what it sounds like. Conferencing is important to writing because it gives you a chance to correct or add things to your writing before you do the final draft.
>
> —Caty, age 12

The professional literature we have read and our experiences in the classroom have shaped our views of what conferencing is and what it is not. Conferencing is not editing. It is not marking a piece of writing with a red pen, making corrections for spelling and punctuation. It is not an isolated activity completed by only the teacher. If conferencing becomes what Lucy Calkins (1994) terms "canned and mechanical," then the teacher will not be able to help students grow and develop as writers. Conferencing is a social practice whose goal is to improve not only the written piece but the writer. It is active; it is the co-construction of language; it is discovery.

According to Donald Graves (1994), "The purpose of the writing conference is to help children teach you about what they know so that you can help them more effectively with their writing" (p. 59).

Conferencing with students about their writing is an integral part of the writing process. It occurs at every stage, with students noting strengths and weaknesses through conversations with the teacher and with peers. Because conferencing is such a dynamic part of the writing process, it is difficult to encapsulate the experience for the reader.

This section provides two types of conferencing that emerged in our classrooms after much professional reading and years of classroom experience. One type involves the teacher moving around the classroom as students are engaged in various stages of the writing process. The narrative that begins this chapter illustrates this type of conferencing quite succinctly. The teacher conducts informal conferences by making encouraging comments about the writers' words. This type of conference benefits the individual student as well as the student writers seated nearby. Encouragement is contagious and inspires other student writers to continue writing and to improve their drafts. When the teacher praises one student for the use of a powerful lead, the students seated nearby may be inspired to revisit their leads. This type of conference is a manageable way for teachers to encourage students to reflect on what they are writing and to react to improve their writing.

The second type of conferencing that evolved in our classrooms is a more formal meeting between the student writer and the teacher. Tommy Thomason (1998) states, "Like the therapist does with the client, the writing coach helps the writer to think through a problem, to examine possible solutions, and to decide on a course of action and determine to implement it" (p. 25). This type of conference involves not merely encouraging comments; rather it is a planning session for decisive action. The students seek out the teacher when drafts are complete. The students read their writing aloud while the teacher listens and takes notes, and then responds with praise and questions. The goal is to have the student writers do the speaking; therefore, the teacher asks probing questions that focus on the qualities of effective writing.

In Graves's *A Researcher Learns to Write: Selected Articles and Monographs* (1984), sample questions are provided for teachers that focus students' attention on various factors: voice, need for more specifics, language and organization, progress and change, and audience sense. The probing questions we pose also are influenced by the Pennsylvania System of School Assessment (PSSA) writing guide. This guide focuses on the characteristics of effective writing determined by the state: focus, content, organization, style, and conventions. Following are sample questions we use when conferencing with students:

- What is the focus of this section?
- What do you want the reader to know from this paragraph?
- Do you maintain your focus throughout your writing?
- Are your ideas and information in a logical sequence?
- Do your paragraphs deal with one topic?
- Is your writing organized from beginning to end?
- Can you use dialogue in this section to give the reader a stronger image of the characters?
- Is the dialogue meaningful, moving the writing forward and creating images for the reader?
- Are these details relevant to your purpose?
- Do these details add to the story or confuse the reader?
- Does your lead engage the reader? Why?
- Who are some of the people in this room who would be interested in reading this?
- Do you see any improvements in your writing since your last writing piece?
- Do you use any of the writing techniques taught in class?
- Do you use various types of sentences?
- Do you have complete sentences—not run-ons or fragments?
- Did you edit for spelling errors?
- Did you edit for correct punctuation?
- Did you edit for capitalization?

Questioning during conferencing is significant in helping students develop as writers, yet as Lucy Calkins (1994) warns,

> Questions are not the goal.... I am stressing this point not to devalue the questions we ask, but to empower them. When our questions grow out of our emerging understanding of the writer, they are alive and fresh and powerful. When the same questions grow only out of a chapter on good questions to ask in writing conferences, they quickly become canned and mechanical. (p. 225)

The student writer initiates a conversation with the teacher.

We believe teachers should be aware of the danger of conferencing that becomes "canned and mechanical." The sample questions we provided emerged as we met with our students to discuss their writing. They address topics that frequently appear, but this list is not exhaustive. These questions are springboards for conversation. Once the conversation flows, conferences become individualized according to each student writer's needs. The dynamic nature of conferencing will lead students to improve their writing independent of the teacher.

Assessment of Written Pieces

Although our goal is to share practical approaches to teaching reading and writing that achieve the goal of creating lifelong readers, writers, and learners, assessment must be addressed—despite it not being an "approach." State and local assessment in all subject areas is a reality that policy makers, school boards, parents, and administrators deem essential to evaluating schools' strengths and weaknesses. *Adolescent Literacy: A Position Statement* states that "adolescents deserve classroom assessments that bridge the gap between what they know and are able to do and relevant curriculum standards; they deserve assessments that map a path toward continued literacy growth" (1999, p. 6). Thus, we discuss writing assessment here because it shares this goal with conferencing—to improve the writer.

There are academic standards for reading and writing established by state departments of education in the United States, and students are assessed to determine achievement levels at various grade levels. Students and teachers, therefore, are accountable to meet these standards. We use the Pennsylvania Writing Assessment Scoring Guide as a tool during conferencing, assessment, and instruction. We employ this guide not only because of state assessment, but primarily because it supports our goal of improving the writer.

We have created a rubric based on this guide (see Appendix L), which is a learning tool for teachers and students and supports our goal by making students cognizant of the qualities of effective writing. A major minilesson that begins our school year is training students to use the rubric to assess themselves. Students practice evaluating written pieces, using the rubric in small groups and individually, and discuss the results as a whole class. The teacher and students then focus on how the writer can return to the written piece to revise and to edit. This self-assessment becomes a part of the writing process for students; it generates student autonomy and self-awareness as writers.

Spelling Workshop

Spelling Workshop is a great experience. It is better than writing the spelling words ten times each and trying to remember each of them. Spelling Workshop gives me a memory device for each word. It is also fun making memory devices with my group. We also have pretests that aren't graded. The time between Spelling Workshop and the test gives me time to practice the memory devices.

—Megan, age 12

I think Spelling Workshop really helps me because it is a creative way to help us learn the words better. Instead of writing the words many times, we go over memory devices to help us remember the words. We break into small groups and talk about what devices we could think of using.

—Alison, age 12

Spelling, an integral part of writing, is important but confusing for students. English has been influenced by many languages, making it vocabulary rich; however, this also means that consistent spelling rules are absent. In *A Fresh Look at Writing* (1994), Graves states, "Only 46 percent of words in the English language can be spelled the way they sound; the remaining 54 percent draw on the writer's visual memory of what the words look like" (p. 265). With this in mind, it is important to develop a spelling program that emphasizes visual, auditory, and kinesthetic modes of learning and that offers strategies that "teach how to spell not what to spell" (Rosencrans, 1998, p. 6).

The spelling word lists that we use originate from various sources and include high-frequency writing words, personal spelling demons, most confusing words, words from a topic being studied, and words that follow the basic spelling rules of the English language. In our classrooms, spelling workshop is a 30- to 45-minute block each week. We begin by giving a pretest to activate students' prior knowledge of the spelling words. Next, we discuss and practice some of the strategies we discovered as we researched this topic. We have chosen to emphasize several that focus on the various modes of learning; however, there are many additional strategies that researchers discuss. Strategies can be adapted and modified to meet the needs of students. The key is that they do not rely on mere memorization (*what* to spell); rather, they teach *how* to spell, and can be used well into adult life.

Memory devices. Students are instructed to create memory devices that have personal meaning. For example, when spelling the word *tomorrow*, Teresa explains to her students that she remembers the spelling because her last name, Morretta, has one *m* and two *r*s. Some memory devices can work for many students. For example, when spelling the word *friend*, the teacher can explain "She is my fri*end* to the *end*." This strategy is employed at every spelling workshop and during writing.

Drawing. Students draw pictures to remember the spelling of words that originate from Greek and Latin roots. For example, to remember words that are derived from the Latin root *circum*—such as *circulate, circumference, circular,* and *circumvent*—we discuss the meaning of *around*. Students then connect the meaning of *around* to a labeled sketch of *circle*, which aids them in spelling these new words.

Visualizing. Many researchers discuss this strategy that asks students to write the uncertain spelling of a word several different ways to see if the look of the word helps them decide on the spelling. Students choose the spelling that looks correct to them. Rosencrans (1998) calls this strategy "Looking Good," of which the "goal at this point is simply to have the student understand that correct spellings will often be recognized by the way they look" (p. 49).

Write, Listen, Look, Write. Students fold a piece of paper in half and open it. The teacher dictates a word. Students record the spelling on the left side of the paper. The teacher spells the word correctly aloud. During this auditory clue, students check their spelling with their pencils, pointing to each letter. Students circle any errors in their spelling. The teacher writes the correct spelling on the board while students watch this visual clue. Students copy this spelling from the board onto the paper in the right column. After completing this strategy for all the words in the list, students highlight the words that were misspelled. In small groups students create memory devices to remember the spellings of troublesome words.

Spelling strategies alone do not improve the writer. Spelling becomes meaningful only through daily reading and writing experiences that show how authors need to spell to communicate effectively. A rich print environment supports this. Students recognize that a written piece with many spelling errors interferes with the writer's meaning and the reader's understanding. Although we teach and practice spelling strategies explicitly, the inclusion of real literature and students' writing make this part of language learning relevant to students.

Revisiting Reading/Writing Workshop

We explained the approach and the value of reading/writing workshop in Chapter 3, yet it is necessary to mention it as a practical approach to engage writers as well as readers because students may choose to read or to write at this time. During reading/writing workshop, students have the opportunity to brainstorm, conference, draft, revise, edit, or publish their writing.

The community of writers already extends from the classroom to the school library, other classrooms, and local libraries and bookstores. We further enrich language experiences for writers by providing opportunities for students to have their work published by professional companies. Writing contests are posted and students are encouraged to enter. Two magazines that are written for students by students are *Stone Soup* and *Merlyn's Pen*. *Stone Soup* accepts stories, poems, reviews of books, and artwork. For all submissions, the magazine requires the student's name, age, home address, phone number, and a business-size, self-addressed stamped envelope. For a story or poem, students submit a typed manuscript, a cover letter introducing the student, and the kinds of stories the writer enjoys writing. If students are interested in reviewing a book, they send a cover letter indicating their interest and why, and tell about themselves and the kinds of books they enjoy reading. If students want to submit artwork, they should send samples and a cover letter about the kinds of stories they like to illustrate. Students whose work is accompanied by a self-addressed stamped envelope will hear from *Stone Soup* within 4 weeks. If they want work returned, the envelope must be large enough and have sufficient postage. The address for submissions is *Stone Soup*, P.O. Box 83, Santa Cruz, CA 95063, USA.

Merlyn's Pen focuses on student writers in Grades 6 to 12, and selected authors receive payment. This magazine also requires a double-spaced typed manuscript. Issues of *Merlyn's Pen* include a copy of a cover sheet for submissions that student writers must complete and send with their manuscripts. Students who submit for a response only receive it within 8 weeks—acceptance or rejection. The comprehensive critique takes 10 weeks and gives writers detailed editorial responses. The address for submissions is *Merlyn's Pen*, P.O. Box 910, East Greenwich, RI 02818-0910, USA.

There are many writing contests sponsored by local newspapers and national and international publishing companies. Frequently, writing contests are advertised on the Internet and made known to principals and teachers through mail and workshops. Teachers should seek out writing contests because they expand student writers' sense of community and give them an authentic purpose for writing.

Final Reflection

It is the balanced reading/writing classroom—student-centered, dynamic, and active—that best leads to the development of the community of writers. The use of real literature and students' writing gives authentic purposes for adolescents to recognize that they write for an audience. The language skills taught have real meaning and are relevant to students' as writers and readers.

Teachers show students they value them and their writing by the approaches that are used in the reading and writing classroom. Freewriting demonstrates that writing is valuable because the teacher models the approach and designates class time for it. Conferencing shows that students and their writing are valuable because the teacher provides individual attention to them and their writing. With these approaches, students' self-esteem is buoyed and they become invested in their learning. The adolescent demand for meaningful learning is achieved.

The next chapter depicts how we celebrate the reading and writing connection in our classrooms. This celebration is accomplished by displaying portfolios at a portfolio tea party, having a poetry workshop, and showcasing author studies and student-published books at local bookstores and libraries. Student definitions and sample work appear to illustrate each component of this celebration. Our discussions of these components demonstrate that teachers as well as students celebrate when using the combined approach.

CHAPTER 5

Students and Teachers Celebrating the Reading and Writing Connection

We accept that our purpose as educators is to enable middle school students to become lifelong readers, writers, and learners. The combined approach emerged as the means to achieve this purpose. Our philosophy is based on connecting reading and writing and making learning meaningful, so practices that engage readers and writers develop lifelong readers, writers, and learners. The blank book, author studies, poetry workshop, and portfolios celebrate the reading and writing connection; assist teachers to meet national, state, and local standards; make learning meaningful to students; promote a literacy club; and inspire students to carry the love and appreciation of reading and writing into their adult lives.

Blank Books

A blank book is an empty book with no illustrations and no writing in it. What we do is think of anything we want to write about and make it into a story. After writing a rough draft, we then put it in our book. First, it is revised and edited by my friends and Ms. Ambrosini. I really like making blank books because I get to use my own ideas and I can express myself in my writing and illustrations in the book. Blank books have helped me to be a better writer by helping me to expand my thinking and also letting me know what other people think about my writing. I get all different opinions about it. I learned about many authors and the different styles of writing that they do. It is also fun to come up with my own story as well as characters. Teachers should do blank books because it shows them what their students are learning about writing.

—Kaeleen, age 12

Our students celebrate reading and writing from the very beginning of the school year. A main component of our reading and writing program is the blank book, a hard-back, bound book with blank pages. (We order ours from Treetop Publishing Company, P.O. Box 085567, Racine, WI 53408-5567, USA) These blank pages will be filled with students' words and pictures as they create stories for various audiences. Students are introduced to the blank-book writing assignment during the first week of school, which makes them aware that they are writers for an audience.

To give students a feel for the awesome task of writing a book, they read Janet Stevens's *From Pictures to Words: A Book About Making a Book* (1995). In this picture book, the author explains the stages of the writing process by thinking aloud as she writes a picture book. This book elucidates the recursive nature of the writing process because the author returns to prewriting and early drafts after taking a second look at her work and conferring with her colorful characters. This valuable resource also instructs student writers to rely on personal experiences and imagination as they begin to write for an audience.

Students are now more aware of this writing task. We provide them with a time line for prewriting, drafting, revising, editing, and publishing their text. There are deadlines for each stage of the writing process because students need this structure to help manage a year-long writing piece. Once the school year is underway, they come to recognize that writing is recursive. As we conference with students, they move among the various stages of the writing process. For example, after meeting with the teacher about a completed draft, a student may realize that her main character is flat and not fully described. Teacher and student discuss the ways a writer can create images for readers. The student returns to her prewriting storyboard to recall what made this character worth writing about. Not only is the student conferencing as a part of the revising stage, but she is drafting and revisiting her prewriting. Although the deadlines and steps that are posted for students in our classrooms may appear linear to a classroom outsider, in action the writing process is recursive.

Blank Book Time Line

• Prewriting: Students complete a fiction map, a storyboard, or a clustering/webbing map. Students complete prewriting, brainstorming ideas for their future books. Students typically have September and October to work on this step. We conference with students during reading/writing workshop to monitor their progress; students may also initiate a conference if they feel it is necessary. In place of a minilesson, we provide time during reading/writing workshop for students to discuss their prewriting with their literature groups and brainstorm more ideas.

• Drafting: Students write a first draft. Students use what they learned in prewriting to begin writing the draft of their narrative. Students write for most of November, December, and January, conferencing with teachers and peers throughout this time.

• Revising: Students conference about and make changes to their completed drafts. Students are expected to have two peers read their drafts and respond to their writing before they submit their drafts for a formal conference. Now the students read their drafts aloud as we listen carefully and take notes. Once students finish reading aloud, we share our ideas as listeners and readers of the story. This conference spurs students to write a second draft; students continue to revise after this conference. This step occurs during February.

• Editing: Students type another draft from the revised second draft. Students again have two peers read and edit their drafts, checking for spelling, punctuation, capitalization, and grammar. Students then submit their drafts to us—the final editors. These second revised and edited drafts are due at the end of March.

• Publishing: Students publish their stories in blank books with illustrations (see Figure 8). Students choose how to present the text and illustrations of their books. The published books are due at the beginning of May to be displayed and read by other students in our schools. These books are also displayed at local bookstores and libraries.

Figure 8
Page From a Student's Blank Book

Again Eleanor stopped to see the kitten and again she was late. When the bell rang, Eleanor was only five minutes away. She quickly got to the classroom and opened the door. Mr. Swavinski was not there. Neither was the class.

"Oh, our class is at gym," Eleanor remembered.

She threw down her coat and bag and rushed to gym. Miss. Lindsay was taking role.

"Well, hello, Eleanor, so glad you could join us," Miss. Lindsay said with a smirk.

Eleanor sat down and started on her exercises.

Author Studies

> In an author study a reader picks two different books by the same author and reads them. I like my author study because I can compare the two books and see their similarities. It helps me as a reader by showing me how the same author writes about different settings. It helps me as a writer by giving me ideas for stories I am writing. My author study makes me want to read and it helps me find out about the types of books that are out there.
>
> —Anthony, age 13

Another celebration of the reading and writing connection that occurs at the conclusion of the school year is the students' author studies. Students select an author of young adult literature and read two to four novels by this author. After students choose their authors and

Figure 9
Poster Board With Author Information

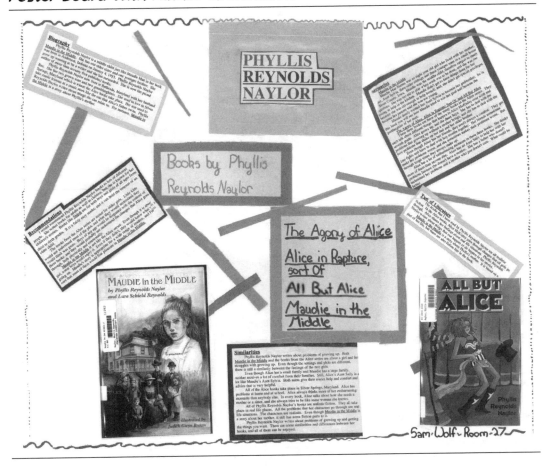

books, we conference briefly with them about their selections. The number of books to be read depends on the individual student's ability.

Students have class time during 2 weeks to read their novels. Students also are required to read at home. Students plan their reading schedule on a chart to manage this reading and writing. As they read in class, students complete a daily reader-response journal entry. During the last 2 weeks of this unit, students respond to the books in writing—doing critical analysis, noting personal reflections, comparing and contrasting, compiling biographical information, and summarizing. Students then display their writing on poster boards, highlighting their authors (see Figure 9). Their work is displayed in our schools and in local bookstores.

The written component of author studies involves the following parts: a biographical sketch of the author, summaries of each book read, a recommendation of the author, an analysis of the books' genres, and a comparison of the books read in reference to the author's style.

Poetry Workshop

Writers

We are writers.

We write about,

Princes, Princesses,

And more.

We think of just about anything,

To write.

We create worlds,

For children,

To dream, read,

And explore.

We are the dreamers,

And we are the writers.

—Ellen, age 12
(written during poetry workshop)

The reading and writing connection is also celebrated in poetry workshop. We formed our poetry workshop after reading the following books: *A Celebration of Bees: Helping Children to Write Poetry* by Barbara Juster Esbensen, *The Reading/Writing Teacher's Companion: Explore Poetry* by Donald Graves, *Wishes, Lies, and Dreams* by Kenneth Koch, and *With a Poet's Eye* by Jane McVeigh-Schultz and Mary Lynn Ellis.

We begin by showing students examples of literary devices employed by poets in both classic and contemporary poetry. Next, we discuss with students how particular figures of speech embrace the reader by evoking images through the poet's words. Although we explicitly teach literary devices such as simile, repetition, and personification, our focus in poetry workshop is having students write poetry. Once students are aware of the various literary devices poets use, they write poems—though they are not required to include the devices in their poetry. The following student poem shows the influence of various literary devices:

Rain Sounds

Trickle

Trickle

BOOM

BOOM

Trickle

Trickle

BOOM

BOOM

Footsteps

Coming

Coming

Is that

A knock at the door?

Tap

Tap

Rain Sounds

—Alexandra, age 12

We run poetry workshop for 8 to 10 class periods. Each class period has a different focus to inspire the student poets. For example, from *With a Poet's Eye*, we have constructed a workshop that utilizes music. We choose six songs without words that create different moods for listeners. A song is played as students listen with their eyes closed. Students then jot down whatever comes to mind—words, images, ideas—as the song is repeated. Then in literature groups, students share their responses. The song is played again as students now compose poems. Students volunteer to read aloud their poems. (Another workshop follows a similar pattern, but instead of musical selections, postcards or artwork are presented and students compose poems in response to these.) The following student poem shows the influence of this music-themed poetry workshop:

James Brown—The Party

Saxophones are playing

Lights are flashing

Everyone's having fun

Fun and excitement

The band is playing on. . .

No one wants to leave this place

This party has got it going on

—Celia, age 12

A Celebration of Bees: Helping Students to Write Poetry provides teachers with topics and questions designed to elicit student responses that can become poems. These common topics are significant because the author's brainstorming ideas stretch the imagination for writing. For example, students write poems using "mystery slips," colored slips of paper on which common nouns are written. These slips are then placed in a pile. Another sheet of colored paper is cut into slips that list descriptive adjectives. Students select one slip from each of the two piles. The resulting combinations inspire creative, imaginative poems. "Furry snowflakes," "nervous sea," and "watery words" are examples of combinations that have emerged. Students are expected to use the combination together at least once in the poem. Again students share their poems with their response groups and then aloud with the whole class. The following student poem uses the combination "secretive mountains":

An Uncharted Place

Where am I?

This isn't familiar.

I've been around the world.

I must be

In Secretive Mountains

That have just unfurled.

—Jeff, age 12

The following student poem uses the combination "dark umbrella":

Raindrops

The dark umbrella shields my face.

Raindrops rolling and bouncing off of

it.

As I walk down the street I hear,

drip drop

drip drop

The raindrops make ripples in

puddles.

After they jump off of my dark

umbrella.

—John, age 13

Sharing and responding to poetry are essential steps in poetry writing because students begin to recognize what constitutes good poetry and what elements they find striking as listeners, readers, and writers. Students talk about the following questions adapted from Donald Graves's *The Reading/Writing Teacher's Companion: Explore Poetry*.

- What struck you about the poem?
- What particular words created interesting images for you?

- Which words did you especially like?
- Did any of the poet's words make you wonder about something?
- What do you think the poet was thinking when he or she wrote the poem?

These questions elevate student responses beyond "I like it" or "It's OK" to thoughtful reflections about the writing and the specific techniques the writer employed. This makes the student cognizant that the poet writes for readers.

Mary Lynn Ellis, coauthor of *With a Poet's Eye*, discusses how to "polish" a poem in poetry workshops. For one or two workshops, students focus on revising and editing their poems. A discussion of how poets structure their poems begins this workshop: why they end lines as they do, why they place certain words alone on lines, why they use particular punctuation marks, and why they may use no punctuation. Students are instructed to find a quiet place where they read their poems aloud to themselves so they can form their poems the way they want readers to "hear" them. Students then read their poems to a partner and a peer conference ensues. The questions from Graves focus students during this conference as does the workshop on revision.

The poetry workshop concludes with students publishing their own poetry books and a class poetry anthology. In addition, students participate in a poet study, reading poetry and looking at what poets do as they write. We begin by discussing in a minilesson what makes certain poems richer experiences for readers, but we acknowledge that the meaning derived from poems is personal. The following poetry collections include contemporary and classic poets: *Poetry for Young People: Emily Dickinson*, *Poetry for Young People: Robert Frost*, *A Dream Keeper and Other Poems*, *Everywhere Faces Everywhere: Poems*, *Joyful Noises*, and *Ordinary Things: Poems From a Walk in Early Spring*.

To complete the poet study we use jigsaw cooperative learning groups. In jigsaw cooperative learning groups, students begin in home groups, which are small groups that work to achieve a common goal. Each home group member has a specific job and is responsible for finding the information the group needs to reach its goal. The home group then splits; each member joins an expert group made up of students with similar jobs. Each expert group member will eventually return to the home group to share what has been learned.

In the poet study, small groups of students become experts for one of the poets. In expert groups, students read their poet's collection and then discuss their personal reactions to the poet. In an informal sharing, each home group member discusses his or her expert group's ideas, thoughts, and reactions to the poet and the poetry. Students share favorite poems by their poets as well. The teacher circulates from group to group, joining the conversations. Our goal is that students take aesthetic stances as they read and respond to poetry, searching for meaning, building on their own interpretations, and expanding them to include the varied interpretations of others. This is another example of reading, as Wilhelm (1997) purports, as a "social practice and a search for meaning" (p.17).

Portfolios

> My portfolio is the place where I put and keep work that is important to me. It holds my work from the beginning of the year and it shows how I improved as a writer since then. My portfolio has the work I am most proud of, too. I can show it to my parents and they can see how I have changed as a reader and writer since September.
>
> —Timothy, age 13

In the reading and writing classroom, the major learning objectives are that students experience and respond to literature and learn to write for an audience. Portfolios affirm that students make reading and writing connections.

Portfolios are collections of students' work selected by them and their teachers to showcase in-process and finished work. Portfolio assessment develops students' metacognition as they choose what to include from all subject areas. Portfolio assessment also offers feedback about student progress and enables teachers to communicate this progress to others.

Teachers determine the criteria and objectives for portfolio selection based on district reading and writing standards, state standards, and professional groups such as the International Reading Association and the National Council of the Teachers of English. Teachers are mindful, too, of students' affective and social domains when determining objectives for portfolios. The objectives will not encompass all the instructional goals designated for a particular grade level. Rather, as

Herman, Aschbacher, and Winters (1992) assert, the criteria teachers decide on for portfolios "should aim at your major learning objectives for students" (p. 24).

An example of a cognitive objective that students are asked to include is "The student will provide a piece of writing that shows that he/she can punctuate dialogue." The teacher has provided many opportunities in writing assignments to use dialogue, so students have several pieces from which to choose. Students are also required to "provide a piece of work that demonstrates understanding of the four elements of a novel." The reading of various genres and the critical analysis of them affords students several pieces of work from which to choose. These objectives come primarily from the school district's curriculum.

An example of an affective objective that students are asked to include is "Show a piece of work that makes you feel proud." This aspect of portfolios builds students' self-esteem, develops students' pride in their work, encourages valuing learning, and gives the observer a fuller picture of the students as learners.

An example of a social objective included in portfolios is "The student will provide evidence of cooperative group work." This piece of portfolios demonstrates the value of working as a team, a key to being a productive citizen.

Before students make permanent decisions about what to include in their portfolios, they must complete entry slips that require them to explain their choices. Entry slips promote metacognition as students think about their choices, their learning, and their thinking. In addition to entry slips, students are asked to evaluate themselves and their portfolios at the halfway point of the school year. During this reflection using the Student Portfolio Review and Evaluation form (see Appendix M), students write about their accomplishments, their learning, and their weaknesses, and they set reading and writing goals for the remainder of the school year. As a final reflection in June, students complete the Portfolio Reflection Letter (see Figure 10 on page 72 and Appendix N). These letters serve as road maps for anyone looking through the portfolios. These reflective elements show that students think about and evaluate their work.

The crux of portfolio assessment is the portfolio conference between teacher and individual student. These conferences occur three or four times during the school year. At the conference the teacher and student discuss their choices, what was accomplished during the

Figure 10
Portfolio Reflection Letter

Dear Reader,

My name is Kerry Brodziak. I was born in South Africa and moved to America when I was four. I have lived in Virginia, Illinois, Wisconsin, and now Jenkintown, Pennsylvania. I enjoy basketball, soccer, field hockey, swimming, reading, and traveling. I play the piano too. When I grow up, I want to be a photographer.

I feel that my strengths in reading are that I pick good books to read and I enjoy them. In writing I am good at putting detail in it. Ever since I started sixth grade my spelling has improved. I now know the difference between their, there, and they're! I have improved in standing up straight and speaking loud enough in public speaking. I have learned in sixth grade how to type faster and how to use a Mac. Using a computer for almost all my projects is what has helped me in that area. When I am given a direction, I listen and stay focused.

I need to work on keeping a good focus in my writing. Sometimes my sentences are awkward. When I am copying notes that Ms. Morretta is dictating, I need to concentrate on writing only the important parts. I also need to remember how to save my work on a disk because I always end up asking someone for help.

When I work in a group, I feel that I work well. Although I do find that I work more quickly when I work by myself, when I work in a group, I enjoy discussing things that have confused me. My group members also give good ideas in stories, and they help me edit my work too.

The thing that I am most proud of in my portfolio is my author study. I am proud of my Author Study because I worked very hard on getting my book read on time. I am also proud of the way I wrote my summaries, so that the reader would want to read the book. It was also so fun to work on.

As you go through my portfolio, you will see work that I have done in all three trimesters. The first thing you will see is a sheet that lists the books I have read in Ms. Morretta's class. You will also see a sheet of my developments that Ms. Morretta wrote. My work is divided up into packets, first trimester, second trimester, and third trimester. They will include things like my first show-not-tell piece of writing, book reports, my double entry journal, a published free write, my first illustrated book and much more!! As you look around the room, you will also see my author study, my blank book, and my last book report. Enjoy!!

Sincerely,

Kerry Brodziak

particular period of instruction, what was learned, what areas still need improvement, and the reading and writing goals for the next marking period.

Portfolios document the change and growth of students as readers, writers, and learners as the school year progresses. Growth as a writer incorporates knowledge about one's self as a writer, awareness of one's strengths and weaknesses, progress in revising for purpose and in publishing with purpose and audience in mind. Growth as a reader is obvious, too; students increasingly take efferent and aesthetic stances toward texts, connecting texts to their own lives, raising questions about what they are reading, and discussing various interpretations. This growth is elucidated throughout portfolios that include double entry journals, dialogue journals, book reports, and author studies. Portfolio assessment develops the whole student, cognitively, socially, affectively, and metacognitively, and showcases students as readers, writers, and learners.

The portfolio tea party, held in May, is the celebration of students' roles as readers who write and writers who read. Students invite parents, former teachers, principals, and the superintendent to review their portfolios. The portfolios are displayed, and refreshments are provided and served by students who also circulate to answer questions about their work for the guests.

Final Reflection

Blank books, author studies, poetry workshop, and portfolios are celebrations for students and teachers. They ensure that the reading and writing connection is apparent and that learning is meaningful for adolescents. The community of readers and writers—the literacy club—is thriving: Students are talking about books and about writing, sharing their reading and writing with numerous audiences, and developing their identities as readers who write and writers who read. Reading and writing have been meshed into the students' lives.

Afterword

What are the elements that make a difference in a successful learning environment? The teacher and the method of teaching. It is the approach that a teacher adopts and its implementation that build lifelong learners. There is no one "right" way to teach reading and writing; however, as teachers of reading and writing, it is indisputable that we must be readers and writers ourselves. The literacy community cannot thrive unless the teacher is a real and visible member: reading, writing, setting goals, conferencing, reflecting, discussing, and sharing.

This book offers our way—a combined approach uniting aspects of explicit instruction and whole language—to teaching language in middle school that has brought our students success. To help students become lifelong readers, writers, and learners, teachers must engage, inspire, and celebrate their students. Once students are engaged in reading and writing they are inspired to read and write. A celebration! In the preceding chapters we provide the practical approaches of the combined approach that engage, inspire, and celebrate our middle school students.

In the middle school reading and writing classroom, promoting meaningful discussions and authentic audiences for writing are ways to engage students. Adolescents thrive on meaningful and authentic activities; they want to know the "whys" of learning. If young adults are not engaged, they will not be motivated to learn. A key element in engaging middle school students is acknowledging the social aspect of learning. They need social interaction to process material as they experience and respond to literature and write for readers. Literature circle groups provide students opportunities to voice their personal interpretations of the text, to voice their connections to their own lives, and to voice their search for meaning. Peer and teacher conferencing enable student writers to reflect on what they have written, which empowers their own writing and invests them in their learning. The practical approaches discussed cannot come to life unless teachers manage the classroom well. Respect for oneself and others and clear expectations are essential for such a dynamic reading and writing middle school classroom.

As middle school educators, we must take on the responsibility to further our education, our knowledge, and our understanding of student learning and adolescent development. Reading professional literature, magazines, and texts and attending workshops and conferences are necessities for teacher growth. Just as we allow for student differences, leaders and decision makers in our schools must acknowledge that teachers instruct using diverse approaches. This will occur when teachers view themselves as learners, read and research topics in education, and develop sound instructional methods.

Reader-Response Journal Questions

What do you notice?

- Do you notice any changes in the personality of the protagonist or antagonist?
- Do you notice any emphasis on an object or minor character that might be important later?
- Do you notice any repeating patterns in the book?
- Do you notice the significance of the title in the chapter you are reading?
- Is there anything unusual about the book's beginning or ending?

What do you question?

- Do you question any of the decisions that a character has made?
- Do you wonder what a certain passage in the book might mean? How do you explain this passage?
- Do you question whether the author realistically presented a certain part of the book?
- Do you question if something that happened in the author's life might have influenced the writing of this novel?

What do you feel?

- Does any part of this section make you feel scared, annoyed, sad, frustrated, happy, or horrified? Which part and why?
- Do you feel differently now about a character or situation in the novel than you did before? Why have your feelings changed?

What do you relate to?

- Does anything in this section remind you of something from your own experience, a movie, a TV program, a song, or another book you have read? Talk about that relationship.

From Berger, L.R. (1996). Reader response journals: You make the meaning...and how. *Journal of Adolescent & Adult Literacy*, *39*(5), 380–385.

Literature Circles:
Teacher Reflection Sheet

+ Well Done   / Average   - Needs Improvement

Literature Circle Meetings: Observations of Student Participation

	1st meeting	2nd meeting	3rd meeting	4th meeting
Asks questions thoughtfully				
Listens actively to others				
Responds thoughtfully to others				
Makes predictions				
Retells the story				
Responds to the author's craft of writing				
Uses the text to support ideas or opinions				
Responds to the elements of literature				
Completes role assignments				
Reflects on reading				
Cooperates with group				
Stays focused				

APPENDIX C

Literature Circle Evaluation: Cooperative Learning Reflection Sheet

During my group's meeting, I participated

more than others   just the right amount   a little bit   not at all

My strongest contribution to my group's meeting: I said,

_____

_____

The strongest contribution of a group member was when _____ said,

_____

_____

For the next meeting, my group should work on

_____

_____ to make our meeting better.

My role in the next meeting is _____ for page _____ to page _____.

Group members' signatures: _____

_____

_____

_____

Word Finder

Name: _____   Group: _____

Book: _____   Page: _____ to page:_____

The word finder's job is to look for special words in the book. These words may be *new, interesting, different, important, strange, hard, funny,* etc.

Write words here that you want to talk about.

Word	Page	Any help given with meaning?	Why you picked it	Definition

At your literature circle meeting, discuss the following for each word:

• How does the word fit the story?

• Do you know what this word means?

• What does this word make you feel or think of?

• Can you draw the word? What would you draw?

• Look up the word and write the definition.

Adapted from Daniels, H. (1994). *Literature circles: Voice and choice in student-centered classrooms.* York, ME: Stehnouse.

Discussion Director

Name: _____   Group: _____

Book: _____   Page: _____ to page: _____

The discussion director's job is to write down questions that you think your group would want to talk about or debate. (Remember to create open-ended questions that require more than a one-word or yes or no response.)

1. _____
   _____
   _____

2. _____
   _____
   _____

3. Why _____
   _____
   _____
   _____

4. How _____
   _____
   _____
   _____

5. If _____
   _____
   _____
   _____

Adapted from Daniels, H. (1994). *Literature circles: Voice and choice in student-centered classrooms*. York, ME: Stehnouse.

Passage Picker/Summarizer

Name: _____   Group: _____

Book: _____   Page: _____ to page:_____

The passage picker's job is to choose parts of the book to read aloud to the group. These parts can be a good description, a funny section, a scary part, an interesting part, an example of good writing, or a part that is important to the story—it also may show foreshadowing, mood, or conflict.

Parts to be read aloud at the literature circle meeting:

Page	Paragraph	Why I like it

At your literature circle meeting:

- Read each of the paragraphs you have chosen.

- Discuss why you like it.

- Ask your circle members for their opinion.

- Ask group members to assist you as you write the summary of this section on the back of this paper.

Adapted from Daniels, H. (1994). *Literature circles: Voice and choice in student-centered classrooms.* York, ME: Stehnouse.

APPENDIX G

Connector

Name: _____ Group: _____

Book: _____ Page: _____ to page: _____

The connector's job is to find connections between the book and the world you live in. This means connecting what you read to any of the following: your own life, events at school or in your neighborhood, events you have heard about on the news, similar events on television or in movies, people you know, and other books or stories.

This section reminds me of

1. _____

Why? _____

_____

2. _____

Why? _____

_____

3. _____

_____

Why? _____

_____

4. _____

Why? _____

_____

Adapted from Daniels, H. (1994). *Literature circles: Voice and choice in student-centered classrooms.* York, ME: Stenhouse.

Sample Literature Circle: A Whole-Class Reading of *The Cay* (Realistic Fiction)

The Cay by Theodore Taylor

Phillip Enright, an 11-year-old American boy, lives with his parents on the island of Curacao during World War II. When the threat of the war reaches the island, Phillip and his mother journey back to the United States. On the way, their ship is torpedoed by a German submarine. As they evacuate the ship, Phillip and his mother are separated after he is hit on the head. Phillip's companions become Timothy, an old native islander, and Stew Cat. Phillip contends with blindness, being stranded on a cay, and the prejudices that he feels toward Timothy.

Objectives

- To recognize *The Cay* as an example of *realistic fiction* by noting many examples of the characteristics of realistic writing.
- To explain the *change* in Timothy and Phillip's relationship as the novel progresses by noting, discussing, and analyzing the *conflicts* between them.
- To analyze the reasons for Phillip's *prejudice* against Timothy; to discuss various reasons for prejudice in modern society.
- To describe Phillip's maturing from childhood to adulthood citing key *conflicts* that lead to this *rite of passage*.
- To identify the *theme* of the novel; to recognize the events that the author uses to share the message about life.

Before reading

The teacher may choose from among the following:

1. Role-playing activity

   - Students work in pairs. One partner is blindfolded and is led around the room by the other partner. The blindfolded partner then walks for a minute alone around the room. The partners next switch roles. The blindfolded partner is now asked to smell certain scents and to identify them. The blindfolded partner also is asked to taste an unknown sweet (chocolate).

- Small groups: students are asked to describe how being blindfolded was different from being able to see.

2. View a scene from the movie *Scent of a Woman*
- Background to the movie: Frank, a retired military leader, is blind. Charlie is a young student who is stranded with Frank in New York City—an unknown place.
- View a 10-minute scene from the film. Students focus on the abilities of Frank. What observations can Frank make even though he is blind? How does he do this? What are the differences between Frank and a sighted person in this situation?

3. Students learn about the geography of Central America and South America.
- As a class, locate Venezuela, Curacao, West Indies, Caribbean, Holland, Amsterdam, and the United States (Virginia and Pennsylvania) on a map.

4. Island Inquiry Project: Students, individually or in group, choose an island for study.
- Students create 10 questions that focus on the island's history, climate, animal life, plant life, people, customs, and food.
- Students bring resource materials to commence research.
  —Students take notes on index cards.
  —Students compose an outline of their research using the index cards.
  —Students write a rough draft using the outline.
  —Teacher distributes handout that shows proper citation formats.
- Students create a visual presentation of their research. Students choose what visual method to use: poster, diorama, speech, newspaper, etc.
- Students write a final draft of their research paper.
- Students present their research to the class.

5. World War II: K-W-L chart
- Teacher discusses
  —the setting, using a world map
  —the book's relationship to World War II
  —what was going on between the Allied and Axis Powers in 1942
  —the role of U-boats in World War II (shows pictures)
  —the definition of torpedo, oil refineries, and dikes

During reading (Text reading and literature circle discussions)

Chapter 1: Read aloud.

Chapter 2: Read with partner.

Chapter 3: Read aloud with teacher/audio tape. Complete "Timothy's Words" paper in literature circle as chapter is read aloud.

Focus points (on chart):

- characters (Phillip, mother, Timothy) and their conflicts—internal and external
- foreshadowing—pp. 22–24
- elements of realistic fiction

Students' roles:

- (one per group) character map for Phillip
  character map for Timothy
  character map for parents
  word finder

- (individually) reader-response journal entry
  chapter check—monitors student comprehension

Literature circle meeting:

Students

- share character maps
- share word finder
- read journal entries to group
- discuss conflicts and realistic
  fiction elements

Teacher

- observes behavior using checklist

Teacher revisits novel—character webs, elements of realistic fiction, foreshadowing, conflicts, character traits:

- Teacher makes webs for characters on poster paper.
- Teacher asks for examples of elements of realistic fiction.
- Teacher rereads key excerpts from pp. 36–39 from Chapter 3. Using a conflict graphic organizer, teacher and students complete details about this external conflict. Students find words and phrases that show the conflict. The class discusses how the conflict may be resolved.
- Teacher asks students to predict other possible conflicts.

- Language learning connection: Teacher uses the novel as a language-learning tool instead of using a grammar textbook at various intervals throughout the reading of the text.
  —Review direct and indirect objects using sentences from the novel on a transparency.
  —Locate examples of simple and compound sentences.

Chapters 4 and 5: Read independently.

Chapters 6 and 7: Read aloud with teacher.

Focus points (on chart):
- Major event that changes Phillip's life
- Phillip and Timothy's relationship—conflicts
- Author's writing style: Phillip feels and listens because he can't see. Note how the author "shows and not tells" on pp. 47–48 that Phillip is feeling and listening.
- Why Timothy is angry with Phillip
- How does Phillip feel when Timothy leaves him alone on the island?

Students' roles:

(one per group)	character map for Phillip
	character map for Timothy
	conflict paper
	word finder
(individually)	reader-response journal entry
	chapter check

Literature circle meeting:

Students	Teacher
• share character maps (any changes?)	• observes behavior using checklist
• share word finder	
• read journal entries	
• discuss conflicts using conflict paper	

Teacher revisits:
- major events and conflicts
- author's writing style: words that reflect Phillip listening and feeling more (pp. 47–49)
- elements of realistic fiction
- character traits

Chapter 8 and 9: Listen to audio tape or partner read.

Chapter 10: Read aloud with teacher; students take parts.

Focus points:
- climax of the story—turning point in Timothy and Phillip's relationship; foreshadowing (page 70)
- Chapter 9—page 76 (Timothy slaps Phillip; Phillip asks Timothy to be friends; Timothy says they've always been friends)
- theme—message of the book

Conflicts: external or internal

Students' roles:
- (one per group)   word finder
                     conflict paper
- (two per group)   elements of realistic fiction
- (individually)   reader-response journal entry
                     chapter check-up

Literature circle meeting:

Students
- share conflict paper
- share word finder
- elements of realistic fiction
- read journal entries
- share how Phillip has changed
- discuss theme

Teacher
- observes behavior using checklist

Teacher revisits:
- story pyramid; climax
- discuss how Phillip is changing
- elements of realistic fiction
- theme

Movie—*The Ernest Green Story*

1. Introduce the movie with newspaper article and description of movie on transparency. Read the newspaper article aloud.

2. Watch movie.

3. Complete handout about movie independently. Discuss the handout in literature circles.

4. Watch *Oprah* episode that features the Little Rock Nine.

Chapters 11 and 12: Read aloud with teacher discussing focus points.

Chapters 13 and 14: Read independently or with partner.

Chapter 15: Read aloud with teacher—very dramatically.

Focus points:

- Chapter 11—"jumbi" experience and Phillip's reaction to Timothy's superstition
- Chapter 12—How has Timothy and Phillip's relationship changed?
- Chapter 15—events of the falling action

Students' roles:

- (one per group)   word finder
  conflict paper
  elements of realistic fiction
  chart the falling action
- (individually)   reader-response journal entry
  chapter check-up

Literature circle meeting:

Students

- share conflict paper
- share word finder
- elements of realistic fiction
- discuss p. 70 as foreshadowing of Timothy's death
- falling action events
- read journal entries

Teacher

- observes behavior using checklist

Teacher discusses

- Choice of extension project:
  —collage: depict what Phillip learned from Timothy as a person and about survival
  —music: find a song that shows the theme of respect for all people; give a brief summary of song and its meaning; discuss how song fits theme; give opinion of song/songwriter/singer
  —poem: write a poem that explains Phillip's blindness and illustrate it

Chapters 16, 17, 18, and 19: Read independently or with a partner.

Focus points:
- falling action, conclusion
- theme

Students' roles:
- (as a literature circle group)   Find four details from novel (scenes, actions, dialogue) that support the theme. Put theme in center of drawing paper and illustrate the details.
- (individually)   reader-response journal entry

Literature circle meeting:

Students
- read and discuss journal entries
- discuss falling action and conclusion
- complete prewriting story map as a group for book report

Teacher revisits:
- Discuss the theme of novel using students' theme project
- Discuss examples from the book that show how the novel is realistic fiction
- Discuss story map
- Discuss book report and due date

After reading
- Show *People*—movie based on the book by Peter Spier

APPENDIX I

Sample Literature Circle: Student-Selected Texts Within Science Fiction Genre

Objectives:
- To read and to comprehend a science fiction/fantasy novel.
- To recognize and to discuss the characteristics of science fiction/fantasy stories.
- To work cooperatively in literature circles (Each student will perform each role—discussion director, passage picker/summarizer, connector, word finder—once).
- To write a book report that evaluates the novel as an example of science fiction/fantasy.

Before reading (choosing a book)
- Students read the synopses of five novels: *The Devil's Arithmetic* by Jane Yolen, *The Hobbit* by J.R.R. Tolkien, *Interstellar Pig* by William Sleator, *The Lion, the Witch, and the Wardrobe* by C.S. Lewis, and *A Wrinkle in Time* by Madeline L'Engle.
- Students decide on top two preferences.
- Teacher assigns students to literature circle.

During/after reading
- Novel is divided into four parts. Repeat this schedule for each part:
    Two or three days for reading and role assignment
    - reading and role assignment sheets or other literature study choices
    One day for literature circle meeting
    - all groups meet to perform roles and teacher records students' participation by rotating to each group for about 5–10 minutes, using checklist
    - students fill out cooperative learning reflection sheet at the end of class
    - all work is organized in literature folder.

Literature Study Choices

- reading of book (pair reading or individual)
- completing of role assignment

If students finish these two, then they may work on...

- book talk presentation (cooperative oral presentation of the book to the class)
  - —the group decides what they want to present to the class about the book
  - —the group plans the book talk to flow in an organized manner
  - —the group plans how to present the book using visual aids (about 5 minutes)
  - —time your presentation!
- Book report (individual writing, critical thinking about the book)

Grading/assessment/requirements

1. Literature folder

• role assignment sheets	25 points
• literature circle evaluation/ cooperation reflection sheets	25 points
• book talk	25 points
• teacher reflection on literature circle meetings	25 points
	100 points

2. Book report | 100 points

APPENDIX J

Sample Literature Circle: Student-Selected Texts Within Nonfiction Genre

Objectives:

- To read and to comprehend a nonfiction text—autobiography/biography.
- To learn about the Holocaust—World History.
- To work cooperatively in literature circles (each student will perform each role—discussion director, passage picker/summarizer, connector, word finder—once).
- To write a book report that evaluates the novel as an example of a nonfiction text.

Before reading

1. During SSR the children will read *Anne Frank: Beyond the Diary: A Photographic Remembrance*.

2. Read aloud the picture book *The Children We Remember* by Chana Byers Abells to create the atmosphere and establish how Jewish people's lives changed under Hitler's reign.

3. Complete a K-W-L chart as a class on the chart tablet about WWII, Hitler, and the Holocaust.

4. Students will explore the time/place of these books by jigsaw cooperative learning groups through research (handout provided) and visit Internet sites for enrichment after research; fill in vocabulary page as researching.
   —Expert groups
   - mapping the countries involved in World War II
   - Jewish experiences during World War II
   - Hitler and his defeat

5. Students will go back to home groups and complete a newspaper article on the three topics. Each expert writes an article and the group puts it together as a newspaper.

6. Read aloud handout (pages 22–23) from "Thematic Unit: World War II," *Teacher Created Materials Incorporated*, by Julie R. Strathman, to pull all research together.

7. Read aloud *Terrible Things* by Eve Bunting, discussing how this book relates to the study of the Holocaust.

8. Show movie *New York Times Lives From the Past—The Seeds of the Holocaust 1933 to 1935* Module 1. Show movie *New York Times Lives From the Past—The Death Camps 1935 to 1945* Module 2 is shown midway through this unit. Show movie *New York Times Lives from the Past—The Trial of Adolf Eichmann 1961* Module 3 as a conclusion to the unit.

Choosing a book

- Students read the synopses of four novels: *Upstairs Room* by Johanna Reiss, *We Are Witnesses: Five Diaries of Teenagers Who Died in the Holocaust* by Jacob Boas, *Rescue: The Story of How Gentiles Saved Jews in the Holocaust* by Milton Meltzer, *Hiding to Survive: Stories of Jewish Children Rescued from the Holocaust* by Maxine B. Rosenberg.
- Students decide on their top three preferences.
- Teachers assign students to a literature circle.

During/after reading

Designate three days for reading and completing student roles. Schedule the literature circle meeting for the fourth day.

Literature study choices

- reading of book (pair reading or individual)
- completing of role assignment

If students finish these two, then they may work on...

- book talk presentation (cooperative oral presentation of the book to the class)
    —the group decides what they want to present to the class about the book
    —the group organizes the book talk to flow in an organized manner
    —the group plans how to present the book using visual aids (about 5 minutes)
    —time your presentation!
- Book report (individual writing, critical thinking about the book)
- Internet Web sites
- Write poems
- Work on portfolio
- Blank book

Grading/assessment/requirements

1. Literature folder
   - role assignment sheets   25 points
   - literature circle evaluation/
     cooperation reflection sheets   25 points
   - book talk   25 points
   - teacher reflection on
     literature circle meetings   25 points
     _____
                                                               100 points

2. Book report   100 points

3. Comprehension test   100 points

APPENDIX K

Sample Literature Circle: Student-Selected Texts Within Nonfiction Genre Using Double Entry Journals

Objectives:
- To read and to comprehend a nonfiction text.
- To learn about slavery and the Civil Rights movement—American History.
- To work cooperatively in literature circles; each student will keep a double entry journal.
- To write a "How to Be" poem that evaluates the novel as an example of a nonfiction text.

Before reading

1. K-W-L chart on Civil War and Civil Rights movement

2. Discuss "liberty and justice for all" by reading *Dear Benjamin Banneker* by Andrea Davis Pickney.

3. Read current articles on slavery and Civil Rights movement. Reference Junior Scholastic, local newspapers, Internet.

4. Discuss the setting and reasons of the Civil War with map on overhead. Read *Pink and Say* by Patricia Polacco and primary sources on slavery (entries of a few slaves) to give the students a feel for the era.

5. Use the video *America's Civil Rights Movement: A Time for Justice.*

6. Use time line on overhead to show the years from slavery into the Civil Rights era.

Choosing a book

- Students read the synopses of four novels (two cover slavery and two cover the Civil Rights movement): *Escape From Slavery: The Boyhood of Frederick Douglass in His Own Words* by Michael McCurly, *Get on Board: The Story of the Underground Railroad* by Jim Haskins, *Witness to Freedom: Young People Who Fought for Civil Rights* by Belinda Rochelle, and *Warriors Don't Cry* by Melba Pattillo Beals.
- Students decide on their top three preferences.
- Teachers assign students to a literature circle.

During reading

- Explicit instruction
—characteristics of history writing
—distribute chart
—using history textbook, find examples of the four characteristics of history writing
—double journal entry
—definition, requirements, and expectations

- Students' roles
—complete double entry journal (all students)
—complete history writing chart (all students)
—word finder (one person per section)
—chapter check-up and character tracking chart are optional

- Schedule
—three days should be designated for reading and completing student roles
—the literature circle meeting can be scheduled for the fourth day

- Literature circle meeting
—The teacher leads the whole class in a discussion that focuses on what history writers do, using a chart.
—Students meet in circles to discuss a summary of what was read; complete double entry journals, and word finder.

After reading

- "How to Be" poem (This poem, an alternative assessment strategy, illustrates students' understanding of the topic or text.)

Grading/assessment/requirements

• Double entry journal	80 points
• Student roles (word finder, history writing, chart, and literature circle discussions)	20 points
	————
	100 points
• "How to Be" poem	100 points

Writing Score Sheet

Name: _____   Group: _____

Revising Skills

Purpose: focus, clear language, exact words, single point of view

2	4	6	8	10
absence of focus	confused focus	vague focus	adequate focus	clear, sharp focus

Organization: makes sense, paragraph deals with one topic, logical order of sequence, beginning and ending are evident

4	8	12	16	20
absence of organization	confused organization	inconsistent organization	appropriate, logical organization	obviously controlled and/or clearly organized

Content: tells enough, details, show not tell, dialogue, ideas developed

4	8	12	16	20
absence of relevant content, ideas not developed, no images	content limited to a listing, repetition, or mere sequence of ideas; few images	sufficient content; more development needed to create images; some images	specific and illustrative content beyond just listing events; images	substantial, specific, and illustrative content; sophisticated ideas that are well developed

Editing/Proofreading Skills

Grammar and sentence structure: complete thoughts, no run-ons or fragments

2	4	6	8	10
Run-ons and fragments so severe that ideas are difficult if not impossible to understand	Run-ons and fragments seriously interfere with the writer's purpose	Repeated use of run-ons and fragments but not severe enough to interfere with writer's purpose	Some run-ons and fragments some varied sentence structure	few run-ons and fragments varied sentence structure—simple, compound, and complex

Usage: subject/verb agreement, pronoun agreement, correct word choice

2	4	6	8	10
Usage errors so severe that writer's ideas are difficult if not impossible to understand	Usage errors seriously interfere with writer's purpose	Repeated usage errors but not severe enough to interfere with writer's purpose	Some usage errors	Few usage errors

Mechanics: capitalization, punctuation, spelling (same descriptors as Usage)

4	8	12	16	20

Final Copy Skills

Handwriting, neatness, following directions

2	4	6	8	10

Total _____

Student Portfolio Review and Evaluation

"I Did It!"

Look through your portfolio and list your accomplishments (what you have done well—name the pieces that show your abilities as a reader or a writer) and things you learned (skills that have made you a better reader and writer) in reading and writing during the first and second quarter of the seventh grade.

List accomplishments:

_____

_____

List things you learned:

_____

_____

Improvement needed...

You still do have some areas that need improvement as a reader and writer. Look through your portfolio, note frequent errors or my comments, and list things in reading and writing you want to and need to work on and improve.

List your goals as a reader and a writer for the third and fourth quarters.

List what you need to improve:

_____

_____

List your goals:

To_____

To_____

To_____

APPENDIX N

Portfolio Reflection Letter

By the time we have the portfolio tea party, you will be required to have a reflection letter written about your learning; this will be like a road map for anyone looking through your portfolio. You will be writing about your strengths and weaknesses. Your response/cooperative learning group will revise and edit the letter before it is published. Please read the following directions about format and requirements.

Your letter will begin with "Dear Reader" and will consist of six paragraphs. Each paragraph will focus on one main idea.

1. Introduction of self

2. What you feel your strengths are in reading, writing, speaking, listening, and the use of technology

3. What you feel you need to work on in reading, writing, speaking, listening, and the use of technology

4. What you feel about yourself as a group member in reference to cooperation and individual responsibility to a group

5. What you are most proud of in your portfolio

6. Conclusion stating what the observer will see when going through your portfolio (think of this as a table of contents)

Note: You should use all your work in your portfolio as well as the drafts that were not published and freewrites in your daily writing journal, literature response journals, and dialogue journals. Use your "I Did It" reflection sheets and your cooperative learning reflection sheets. You have been reflecting on your learning since the beginning of the year. You now have to pull it all together in a letter format.

References

Abells, C.B. (1983). *The children we remember*. New York: Greenwillow.

Alexander, L. (1965). *The black cauldron*. New York: Bantam Doubleday Dell.

Angeletti, P., & De Micheli, A. (Producers). (1992). *Scent of a woman* [Videotape]. New York: Muze, Inc.

Atwell, N. (1987). *In the middle: Writing, reading, and learning with adolescents*. Portsmouth, NH: Heinemann.

Atwell, N. (1991). *Side by side: Essays on teaching to learn*. Portsmouth, NH: Heinemann.

Avi. (1991). *Nothing but the truth*. New York: Avon.

Beals, M.P. (1994). *Warriors don't cry*. New York: Pocket Books.

Berger, L.R. (1996). Reader response journals: You make the meaning...and how. *Journal of Adolescent & Adult Literacy, 39*(5), 380–385.

Berry, J.R. (1996). *Everywhere faces everywhere: Poems*. New York: Simon & Schuster.

Boas, J. (1995). *We are witnesses: Five diaries of teenagers who died in the Holocaust*. New York: Scholastic.

Bolin, F.S. (Ed.). (1994). *Poetry for young people: Emily Dickinson*. New York: Sterling.

Bunting, E. (1980). *Terrible things*. New York: Harper & Row.

Calkins, L.M. (1994). *The art of teaching writing* (2nd ed.). Portsmouth, NH: Heinemann.

Cannon, J. (1993). *Stellaluna*. San Diego, CA: Harcourt Brace.

Collier, J., & Collier, C. (1974). *My brother Sam is dead*. New York: Scholastic.

Daniels, H. (1994). *Literature circles: Voice and choice in the student-centered classroom*. York, ME: Stenhouse.

Esbensen, B.J. (1975). *A celebration of bees: Helping children write poetry.* New York: Holt & Company.

Fleischman, P. (1988). *Joyful noises.* New York: Harper Trophy.

Fletcher, R.J. (1997). *Ordinary things: Poems from a walk in early spring.* New York: Simon & Schuster.

Forbes, E. (1943). *Johnny Tremain.* Boston: Houghton Mifflin.

Fritz, J. (1967). *Early thunder.* New York: Puffin.

Graves, D.H. (1984). *A researcher learns to write: Selected articles and monographs.* Portsmouth, NH: Heinemann.

Graves, D.H. (1990). *The reading/writing teacher's companion: Discover your own literacy.* Portsmouth, NH: Heinemann.

Graves, D.H. (1992). *The reading/writing teacher's companion: Explore poetry.* Portsmouth, NH: Heinemann.

Graves, D.H. (1994). *A fresh look at writing.* Portsmouth, NH: Heinemann.

Greene, J.M. (Producer). (1995). *People* [Videotape]. New York: Lightyear Entertainment.

Guggenheim, C. (Producer). (1992). *A time for justice: America's Civil Rights Movement* [Videotape]. Washington, DC: Guggenheim Productions.

Haskins, J. (1993). *Get on board: The story of the Underground Railroad.* New York: Scholastic.

Herman, J.L., Aschbacher, P.R., & Winters, L. (1992). *A practical guide to alternative assessment.* Alexandria, VA: Association for Supervision and Curriculum Development.

Hinton, S.E. (1967). *The outsiders.* New York: Viking Press.

Hughes, L. (1994). *The dream keeper and other poems.* New York: Knopf.

International Reading Association & National Council of Teachers of English. (1996). *Standards for the English language arts.* Newark, DE: International Reading Association; Urbana, IL: National Council of Teachers of English.

Laneuville, E. (Director). (1993). *The Ernest Green story* [Videotape]. Burbank, CA: Disney Studios.

L'Engle, M. (1962). *A wrinkle in time.* New York: Bantam Doubleday Dell.

Levine, G.C. (1997). *Ella enchanted.* New York: Scholastic.

Lewis, C.S. (1950). *The lion, the witch, and the wardrobe.* New York: HarperCollins.

Lowry, L. (1993). *The giver.* Boston: Houghton Mifflin.

Lytle, S.L., & Botel M. (1996). *The Pennsylvania framework for reading, writing, and talking across the curriculum.* Harrisburg, PA: Pennsylvania Department of Education.

McCurly, M. (Ed.). (1994). *Escape from slavery: The boyhood of Frederick Douglass in his own words.* New York: Random House.

McVeigh-Schultz, J., & Ellis, M.L. (1997). *With a poet's eye: Children translate the world.* Portsmouth, NH: Heinemann.

Meltzer, M. (1988). *Rescue: The story of how gentiles saved Jews in the Holocaust.* New York: HarperCollins Children's Books.

Moore, D.W., Bean, T.W., Birdyshaw, D., & Rycik, J.A. (1999). Adolescent literacy: A position statement. Newark, DE: International Reading Association.

Morrow, L.M., & Tracey, D.H. (1997). Strategies used for phonics instruction in early childhood classrooms. *The Reading Teacher, 50*, 644–651.

O'Dell, S. (1980). *Sarah Bishop*. New York: Scholastic.

Ogle, D.M. (1986). K-W-L: A teaching model that develops active reading of expository text. *The Reading Teacher, 39*, 564–570.

Oliver, M.T. (1995). *Gangs: Trouble in the streets*. New York: Enslow.

Owens, S. (1995). Treasures in the attic: Building the foundation for literature circles. In B.C. Hill (Ed.), *Literature circles and response* (pp. 1–12). Norwood, MA: Christopher-Gordon.

Pinkney, A.D. (1994). *Dear Benjamin Banneker*. Orlando, FL: Harcourt Brace.

Polacco, P. (1994). *Pink and say*. New York: Philomel.

Reiss, J. (1972). *The upstairs room*. New York: Scholastic.

Rinaldi, A. (1991). *A ride into morning: The story of Tempe Wick*. San Diego, CA: Harcourt Brace.

Rochelle, B. (1993). *Witnesses to freedom: Young people who fought for civil rights*. New York: Penguin.

Rol, R. (1992). *Anne Frank: Beyond the diary: A photographic remembrance*. New York: Scholastic.

Rosen, M. (Producer). (1995). *New York lives from the past—The death camps 1935 to 1945 Module 2* [Videotape]. New York: The New York Times Company.

Rosen, M. (Producer). (1995). *New York lives from the past—The seeds of the Holocaust 1933 to 1935 Module 1* [Videotape]. New York: The New York Times Company.

Rosen, M. (Producer). (1995). *New York lives from the past—The trial of Adolf Eichmann 1961 Module 3* [Videotape]. New York: The New York Times Company.

Rosenberg, M.B. (1994). *Hiding to survive: Stories of Jewish children rescued from the Holocaust*. New York: Houghton Mifflin.

Rosenblatt, L.M. (1984). The literary transaction: Evocation and response. *Theory Into Practice, 21*(4), 268–277.

Rosencrans, G. (1998). *The spelling book: Teaching children how to spell, not what to spell*. Newark, DE: International Reading Association.

Routman, R. (1991). *Invitations: Changing as teachers and learners K–12*. Portsmouth, NH: Heinemann.

Routman, R. (1996). *Literacy at the crossroads: Crucial talk about reading, writing, and other teaching dilemmas*. Portsmouth, NH: Heinemann.

Say, A. (1993). *Grandfather's journey*. New York: Houghton Mifflin.

Schmidt, G.D. (Ed.). (1994). *Poetry for young people: Robert Frost*. New York: Sterling.

Sleator, W. (1984). *Interstellar pig*. New York: Puffin.

Smith, F. (1992). *Joining the literacy club*. Portsmouth, NH: Heinemann.

Speare, E.G. (1958). *The witch of blackbird pond*. New York: Bantam.

Stevens, J. (1995). *From pictures to words: A book about making a book*. New York: Holiday House.

Strathman, J.R. (1994). *Thematic unit: World War II*. Westminster, CA: Teacher Created Materials.

Taylor, T. (1969). *The cay*. New York: Avon.

Thirty-five years later: Black and white students reunion—dramatic reunion of the white students who tormented the black students. (1996). In *The Oprah Winfrey Show*. Chicago: American Broadcasting Company.

Thomason, T. (1998). *Writer to writer: How to conference young authors*. Norwood, MA: Christopher-Gordon.

Tolkien, J.R.R. (1937). *The hobbit*. New York: Ballantine.

Viorst, J. (1972). *Alexander and the terrible, horrible, no good, very bad day*. New York: Macmillian.

Wiggle Works Scholastic Beginning Literacy System. (1994). New York: Scholastic.

Wilhelm, J.D. (1997). *"You gotta be the book": Teaching engaged and reflective reading with adolescents*. New York: Teachers College Press.

Yatvin, J. (1991). *Developing a whole language program for a whole school*. Newark, DE: International Reading Association.

Yolen, J. (1988). *The devil's arithmetic*. New York: Puffin.

Zindel, P. (1995). *Doom stone*. New York: Hyperion.

Index

N

O

P–Q

R